COUNTRY
SAYINGS

FRED ARCHER

COUNTRY SAYINGS

FRED ARCHER

ALAN SUTTON

First published in the United Kingdom in 1990 by
Alan Sutton Publishing Limited · Phoenix Mill · Far Thrupp · Stroud
Gloucestershire

First published in the United States of America in 1991 by
Alan Sutton Publishing Inc · Wolfeboro Falls · NH 03896–0848

British Library Cataloguing in Publication Data

Archer, Fred 1915–
Country sayings.
1. English language. Hereford and Worcester dialect:
Worcestershire dialect
I. Title
427.44

ISBN 0-86299-837-9

Library of Congress Cataloguing in Publication Data applied for

Typeset in Bembo 11/14
Typesetting and origination by
Alan Sutton Publishing Limited.
Printed in Great Britain by
Dotesios Printers Limited.

To
Cousin George Hunting
who taught me many of the sayings

Contents

Introduction

When as a boy in Worcestershire I worked with the men they had their sayings about almost everything that concerned the land and country life. In the age in which we live many of these country sayings have been forgotten. I have tried to recall some of the couplets, proverbs or saws which were common on the farms and in the villages. Some have a deep meaning, while others are skittish yet interesting.

I remember an old man saying to me when I was young 'Thee doesn't understand my logic.' He was probably right, for I knew him as a thinking man who used to say, 'Because I've never rubbed my back against a college wall folks things I've got a tile loose!' Maybe I can delve deeply into the meaning of some of these very old sayings. George Ewart Evans wrote a book some time ago called *Ask the Fellows Who Cut the Hay*. In it he emphasizes the need not to ignore the older folk but to study their philosophy.

Out in the fields, the men talked of those things which concerned them in their daily lives, and the sayings reflect the rural nature of life as it was for them then. The weather was a constant topic. The reason is obvious, they worked in the open air. When the weather was wet there were no Wellington boots to keep their feet dry. Heavy hobnailed boots dressed with dubbin and leggings were the only protection.

With no professional forecasting of the weather the countrymen or countrywomen relied on their observation of the things around them. The behaviour of animals, the direction of the wind, the nearness of the hills when the hills were capped with low cloud. So many things were noted.

I used to hear Dad say, 'We shall have a frost, the train sounds hollow.' The Mistle Thrush, when he called, meant rain and so was called the Storm Cock. When the Scarlet Pimpernel bloomed it was good haymaking weather. I am afraid that we seem to have lost the instinct that told us whether it would rain or shine tomorrow. Now we rely on the weather forecast on television, on what the satellite tells the meteorologists. We still constantly talk about the weather.

Working with Tom the stockman in the July hay fields the old maids, or horse flies, would be troublesome. They sucked the blood from man and beast, tormenting the horses as they pulled the mowing machine. Tom would say, 'We shall get some Tempest', a good old word for thunderstorm. He was usually right. When a whirlwind took a cock of hay high into the sky that was another sign of thunder to come. The phases of the moon were also important to country folk. Every calendar and almanac showed them. In my father's time folk used to have their parties in winter when the moon was full – the 'Parish Lantern' provided street lighting for free. Some country folk studied *Old Moore's Almanac* but few took it seriously, relying more on their own judgement. It is said that when Old Moore was dying his grandson asked, 'What shall I write in the almanac, Grandad?' The old man replied, 'Put snow in the harvest', and strange as it may seem it did snow that harvest, and *Old Moore's Almanac* has never looked back.

The village church too was, and is, closely connected with the land. The parson who farmed his glebe, the harvest festival, both were part and parcel of village life. Many parsons had a barometer and some a rain gauge in their vicarage gardens, so in the past the parson was also the one to be consulted on the weather. 'The field is as full of couch grass as Hell is full of Parsons' was a saying said kindly, to remind the parson that he, like the workers on the land, was mortal, he had his temptations, but his role in the community was a central one.

Here was a man who was the Citizens' Advice Bureau of the past: he knew what time the train went to the town, he filled in pension forms, gave character references for those seeking employment and advised on the variety of potatoes that suited the soil in the villagers' gardens. The parson was in charge of religious education at the village school and chairman of the school board. Before the advent of parish councils the vestry meeting, which among other things dealt with Poor Law, was the village parliament. Countrymen who had parish relief depended on its generosity or otherwise. More often than not the farmers employed men who through infirmity were of little use on the land. These men were employed at a lower rate, and the farmers, who were rate payers, figured that they may as well employ them as pay them parish relief.

The Church of England and the Nonconformist Church were a foundation of life for the labouring family, providing charity, such as coal at Christmas. The Nonconformists did more on the social side of life. There were Services of Song, attempts at singing *The Messiah*, Sunday School outings and Christmas parties known as 'Bun Struggles'. The language of the King James Bible was the language of the carter and the shepherd. Many learned to read through reading the Bible, and one can detect words from the parson in some of the sayings of the countryman.

A parson at a neighbouring village first came there in the 1920s. When he rode his tricycle around the parish some of the hobbledehoys (youths) called after him, thinking him to be a cissy. He gave them all a good thrashing. Little did they know he had gained his boxing Blue at Cambridge! He called on one of the farmers for a donation for the church. The farmer said, 'Don't it pay then? Because if it don't pay shut it up.' Later, the same farmer applied for a man as a carter. The master and man met at the farm. 'I shall want a note of your character,' the farmer said. At lunch-time the man went to the local inn where he was told that the farmer was a hard task-master. Later in the day the farmer asked the man if he had got his character. The man replied, 'No, but I have got thine and I'm not taking the job.'

Sunday observance was total when I was a boy. We were only allowed to read the Bible or some religious literature, like the *Sunday Companion*. No bike rides, but chapel three times. I knew a man who gave his pigs enough food on Saturday to last them over Sunday so that he did not have to feed them on the Sabbath. It was said that he also killed his cockerel for treading his hens on a Sunday. It says in Micah: 'The letter killeth but the Spirit giveth life.' These folk of years ago kept to the letter, hopefully they had the right spirit.

Picture market gardeners on a Sunday night in June, sitting on the headland of their strawberry field just waiting for the church clock to strike midnight – then and only then would they begin to pick their strawberries. In the days before the advent of British Summer Time it would be getting light at 2.30. After a mild weekend the asparagus buds would be tall on the Sunday and these men would be eager to start cutting their gras. Maybe they could teach us something today when every day is a working day.

One of the changes I notice in the village today is the difference in the way the farmworker dresses. The whole image of Hodge has changed. In the winter he would be dressed in corduroy breeches, with gaiters known as leggings above his hob-nailed boots. Between the wars many men of the land wore puttees bought from the army surplus shops of the time. The Oxford shirt was a kind of uniform on the land. It was worn without a loose collar on week days but a muffler was worn in winter. At haymaking and harvest men still wore flannel under-shirts under their Oxfords; they used to say that if you took them off you would surely catch cold. Now harvesters go shirtless in the fields. Men wore caps in winter and straw hats in summer. The battered straw hat served a purpose in keeping hay seeds from falling down the back of the neck when the men roped the wagon loads of hay.

Sunday clothes were special. Men wore navy blue suits and light, black boots on Sunday afternoons as they walked the country lanes with their families. The modern farmworker is dressed in a T-shirt and jeans in his garden on Sundays.

Today there is much talk about the dangers of eating animal fat and the harm cholesterol does to the heart. When I was a boy families sat down happily to meals of cider and fat bacon. Large amounts of green vegetables were eaten and men walked behind

The author in 1926 riding Blackbird hooked to the Planet horse hoe

Uncle George Archer

Hay harvesting with a Trapper mowing machine near Wincanton, Somerset, c. 1900

the plough rather than riding on a tractor. Only the very poor of
the parish drank skimmed milk, now it is very popular.

There were elementary rules on health and how to treat illness.
Besides the well-known 'an apple a day keeps the doctor away',
country folk had their own simple remedies. Permanganate of
potash in water was used for cuts and sores, and for a gargle for
sore throats; and when there was a 'flu epidemic Dad poured
carbolic acid over the hot coals on a shovel and blew the fumes
around the house as a preventative.

The medicine cupboard also contained Epsom salts, Glauber
salts, iodine, linseed, liquorice, brimstone, treacle, acorns, cam-
phorated oil and eucalyptus. Most of these remedies have now
been replaced by various drugs. When Shepherd Tidmarsh was ill
he asked me to collect the little yellow flowers of Agrimony for
him, he used this as an infusion to make a kind of tea which he said
stimulated his bladder. Brimstone and treacle was a spring medicine when we were young. For bronchitis country folk took
linseed and liquorice – the linseed was boiled with sticks of
liquorice and the resultant fluid was drunk.

I wonder whether Uncle George's remedy for a youngster with
the bellyache worked, a hot cross bun baked on Good Friday and
kept for a year! Maybe the mould was penicillin, long before its
discovery by Fleming!

The lovely smell of a field of beans in blow, or blossom, is, with
the scent of honeysuckle on the roadside hedge, something
special. Of course the hay field is a perfume of summer days.
'Good hay hath no fellow' is so true. Well made silage when
analyzed is said to contain more feed value than hay, but hay made
from old pasture with all the herbs mixed in it is very different
from the nitrogen-assisted rye grass of today. I remember the vet
saying to me when I was a boy, as he picked up a handful of hay
made from permanent grass from the cow's manger and smelled
it, 'That's as sweet as honey.'

When we first cut the hay with tractor mowing machines the
shepherd was critical. The exhaust fumes puffed from the old
Fordson into the swath. 'The sheep won't eat this hay,' he said.

'Why?' I enquired. 'Because it stinks of paraffin.' He may have had a point there.

The sounds of haymaking and harvest I recall: the switch of the scythe, the sound of whetstone on the blade as it was sharpened, then the chatter of the mowing machine knife, the jingle of the chain harness, the creak of the dry wagon wheels, and the noise of the binder as it kicked the sheaves in rows. The sound of threshing, the machine called the drum saying 'More, more, more', and the smell of the steam engine. I remember tidy hay ricks in a full rick yard, stooks of wheat, oats and barley in rows.

The village pub in the old days was a place where a man could take his bread and cheese and an onion bait and have his pint of cider, which has been called 'Agricultural Brandy'. As they refreshed themselves after coming in from the fields the country-men were quite generous in buying each other drinks; a man who was mean was despised.

Often the sayings from the village pubs were in the form of a greeting of good health. A toast I particularly like is from Gloucestershire and Worcestershire:

I looks towards ya.
(Answer) I catches yer eye.
Reply) I speaks according.
(Answer) I bows and smiles.

An amusing incident happened in the village some time ago. Someone told the village doctor that there was a deer in his hill field at dusk. The doctor shot at what appeared to be a deer but it was a cow crib. It was talked about amongst his neighbours. A man buying rabbit skins came to the Plough and Harrow pub. The customers told him that if he went across the road to the doctor's house, the doctor had a very fine deer skin he would like to sell. The doctor was not amused, but when he went to the pub he found out who started the rumour.

As a youth, much of my time in winter was spent with a gun blazing away at pigeons in the sprout fields. In the wide open spaces of the fields on vale and hill guns were fascinating to me. I had one with me most of the time. Once the stockman said of a lady in the village he swore was wearing two hats 'What sights you see when you have not got your gun!' That made me think! When you have not got your gun, you see, it is then that the covey of partridges will settle on the stubble close to where you work. Dad had lots of guns, including an eight-bore duck gun. He had had a muzzle loader when he was a youth and told me that 'if you want to kill dead on the spot you ram the powder but not the shot'.

Today the sound of the guns at clay pigeon shoots reminds me that cartridges are no longer two pence each. As Tom, our stockman, used to say on hearing the report of a gun when we were thirsty in the hay field, 'There's another barrel empty and I have not had a spot.'

Some of my sayings come from the Forest of Dean. The late Harry Beddington of Cinderford used some delightful words concerning the Foresters. Here in the little pocket of land between the Severn and the Wye folk have always thought for themselves and been independent. They have had to to survive hard times. Harry used to say, 'We have lived too long in the woods to be frightened by owls.' There is a very deep meaning in these words. The foresters can be led but, as the saying goes, 'He won't be druv'. Little upsets in country life would worry most folk, but the natives of the Forest of Dean stand square in adversity and soldier on. Their humour is subtle and the stories they tell are often against themselves. One Forester told me that he had had words with his old schoolmistress. 'You told me one and one make two,' he had said. 'That's correct,' she had replied. 'Well now,' the Forester had said, 'I got married and one and one have made six!' Another Forester describing one of his friends said to me: 'Him haven't been as far as I have and I a' bin nowhere.' I know what he meant, the man he was talking about was a bit of a bragger.

Some younger people will question why these sayings were used a generation or so ago. When village folk had very little book learning they depended on what is described as 'The Oral Tradition', wisdom handed down from father to son. The time to plant and the time to reap the crop is dictated by some of the sayings. Fair Days and Saints' Days were important in the countryman's calendar. Stow Fair, 12 May – plant runner beans and shoot rooks; Pershore Fair, 26 June – finish cutting asparagus; Candlemas, 2 February – plant early peas. It was reckoned to plant shallots on the shortest day of the year and to harvest them on the longest.

Ploughing with horses is now but a memory, though one sees it still at ploughing matches. When the tractor took over, the men who had spent half a lifetime behind the team of horses were given tractors to drive. That was a good thing. A.G. Street in one of his writings said, 'Give me a horse ploughman and put him on a tractor, I'll teach him to drive a tractor if he can plough. It's easier to teach a ploughman to drive a tractor than to teach a tractor-driver to plough.' It's a sobering thought that the shape of the plough, the mould board, the breast and the share have not altered much in the two hundred years since Ransome made the first iron plough.

What was the value of these country sayings? The people in the village I grew up in, who had lived under Queen Victoria, certainly relied on country sayings, proverbs if you like, that they had learnt from their parents. I am sure that many of them stemmed from the need of the cottagers to conserve food and to be careful with their meagre wages. A wet harvest, from where some of the sayings sprung, was a disaster for master and man. 'The dough is run all over the oven,' my Grandmother said when Grandfather's flour from his smallholding had been affected by a wet harvest. One hundred years ago there was plenty of hard wheat coming from Canada but Grandfather remembered life before the Canadian prairies yielded wheat for Britain. He remembered the Irish Potato Famine and stored his potatoes and swedes as if they were gold. 'All is safely gathered in' meant much more to our grandparents.

When Grandfather's pig was to be killed he engaged a pig killer who used to arrive at 6.30 on a winter's morning. The early killing of the pig was necessary because his neighbours could help before they went to work. The pig killer was said to be a very religious man and always put a text from the Bible on his postcard confirming the date and time he would be at Grandfather's. One year he wrote these words: 'I shall come to kill your pig next Monday morning at 6.30. Be ye also ready.'

Some of the men who lived and worked on the farm made qualifications when they spoke of the future. I suppose they thought of the words of the Bible: 'Boast not thyself of tomorrow'. Jim, born in 1870, said to me, 'I shall be eighty-five next birthday if I be spared.' Tom the stockman used to say, 'Next year I shall plant Tripoli onions on my allotment if I'm alive and well.'

Some men had a cutting sense of humour. A friend of mine went to a dance in the next village. An old hunting farmer was at the door in the village hall taking the money. He asked my friend, 'What are you doing down here, Charles?' My friend replied, 'It's a change to come to a dance here.' The farmer replied, 'If you can't find a fox in Ashton Wood, it's no good drawing Beckford Coppice.' Speaking in a riddle I agree, but Percy the farmer knew that Ashton Wood was bigger than Beckford Coppice; he also knew quite a lot about the local talent in the female sex.

A more recent saying was coined by a man who worked for me part-time. The month was May, the day was warm and sunny, and Arthur commented as we went to the fields, 'The barley looks better today Fred.' I agreed, then he said: 'Last week I thought we should have to give it the kiss of life.' He meant fertilizer of course, but only a man who had lived in an isolated cottage on the hill could think this way. His expressions were unique, unadulterated by the modern media. He thought for himself. One of his other sayings was: 'God made some of us good and some of us wicked and I am one of the wicked ones.'

The words 'what is it' came in useful when someone was asked a question they did not want to answer. Alfred was asked what sort of onions he had planted on his holding. He replied, 'Oh, they are those what is it.' He knew quite well what the name of the vegetable was but made out he could not remember. He also used the expression when he was asked if he had seen anyone he knew at the Three Counties Show. He replied: 'I saw Joe Brown, I saw Harry Brown, I saw Miss Brown and I saw her what is it.' 'What on earth do you mean by her what is it?' he was asked. 'Oh, her young chap, her fiancé,' he replied. He was a man who lived close to the soil, he treated his land as a friend. Now that men work the land from the seat of a tractor, never getting their boots muddy, it is so different. When men walked to their work along well-trodden footpaths there was no need for conservationists or the Ramblers Association to be on their guard about the retention of footpaths and bridal ways. The paths ran across the field like sheep tracks. The action of boots could be seen on the turf, it grew short and green as the green of a golf course.

Today, some folk may think that country sayings are irrelevant in the modern world, yet, as George Ewart Evans in his books has done much to emphasize, there is much of value in the oral tradition. I hope in a small way that looking back at yesterday and the sayings of its people will give pleasure to folk in village and in town, and will reveal some of the truths and wisdom in these old country sayings. In *Silver King* we read: 'Oh God, put back thy Universe and give me yesterday.' I would say not all the yesterdays were good but 'Give me the best of yesterday'.

CHAPTER ONE

The Weather

Weather forecasting today has become so sophisticated that the average countryman has lost the ability to predict the weather. I remember the time when Dad would ask the shepherd's opinion whether it was going to rain or shine. When tailing and castrating the lambs the wind had to be in what the shepherd said was a warmer quarter, the south-west. It almost seemed that the shepherd could smell a frost. 'Listen to that train, Master. Don't he ever sound holla.'

It won't rain as long as the wind is in that quarter.

One summer in the middle of haymaking, a season which the men called 'catchy weather', we had a rick of hay about half built, known as 'gay'. The hay in the field known as Clay Furlong had been cut about a couple of days and was about half made. The wireless weather forecast that evening was of rain. Dad and his partner decided to carry the hay from Clay Furlong. The shepherd warned, 'If you carry that hay the rick will fire as sure as eggs.' He added, 'How do they know what weather we are to expect, the townies up in London? It won't rain as long as the wind is in that quarter.' The shepherd built the rick and he told me that there was firegrass in it. At school I had learnt about spontaneous combustion which can occur in material stored in a damp condition. The shepherd was right: the rain stayed away, and the rick did fire after a fortnight. The steam used to rise from the stack until one dinner time it went up in flames. The hay that the fire brigade salvaged was chocolate brown and smelt like tobacco. No good for feed.

I'll be glad when Bright Famous comes out.

I was working with Cousin George with the horses around 2 February, Candlemas Day, planting Telegraph and British Lion peas. These are round seeded varieties and very hardy, we never planted the wrinkled seed until the end of March. It was my job to lead the horse pulling the pea drill.

Those early morning February mists are a memory. Quite often there would have been a frost and George would say to me as we sat in the hedge bottom eating our 'bait', 'I'll be glad when Bright Famous comes out!' I wondered what exactly 'Bright Famous' was until it dawned on me that his corruption of Phoebus was so right. Phoebus, the sun, appeared very briefly on those February days.

It looks black over Bill's Mother's.

On other days when the weather was unsettled George came out with another of his sayings. The clouds were heavy and low in the vale. George said: 'It looks black over Bill's Mother's!' Now where Bill's Mother's was I have no idea but if it looked black over Bill's Mother's we hurried towards the shed and shelter!

There's a few too many on one.

Don't keep it off the ground. Get in the dry. The land needs the rain.

We were both working for Dad. George was known to shelter from the slightest shower. As we stood in the shed it was never long before Dad or his partner, Mr Bailey, arrived. They would see the horse standing under the hedge and no sign of George or me. Finding us sheltering, Mr Bailey would often say 'It looks lighter. It's not raining as fast now.' George would reply: 'There's a few too many on one!' A few too many *what* on one I wondered. He meant too many spots of rain on one person. The rain fell on the corrugated iron roof of the shed and our employers knew that the rain sounded heavy on that roof. How they wished that the shed roof was thatched so that George would not be sheltering!

I do not know whether it was also George who invented the saying when it was raining, 'Don't keep it off the ground. Get in the dry. The land needs the rain', but it was so true for the farmer and countryman.

The rain will spoil the little taters.

This was the shepherd's favourite saying on wet days in early summer. I said to him that I thought the potatoes needed the rain, only to get the sarcastic reply, 'The rain will make the little taters into big ones.'

Three white frosts and then a duck's frost.

There is truth in this old saying. White frosts do not usually mean settled dry weather and when on three mornings in succession we see the hoar frost or rime on the hedges it is often followed by rain – the duck's frost.

It's a weather breeder.

The countrymen I knew were slow to acknowledge the coming of spring. 'I've known it snow on Stow Fair Day (12 May),' one man used to warn me. It is understandable that when we were young we were anxious to herald the spring by planting our fields and gardens earlier than the older folk would have done. My old friend Jim, who lived for over ninety years, used this saying, which I have never heard from anyone else. If we had a fine day in February (it often happens!) and I said to Jim, 'What a lovely day!', he would reply, 'It's a weather breeder. Don't be deceived by one fine day. We shall like enough have snow in May, you see if I'm not right!' What is a weather breeder? It does seem beyond description yet the truth behind the saying is that a weather breeder is a day when the weather is unseasonable; a bright February day does not mean that winter is over. We have all experienced years when the shortest day, 21 December, has been warmer than the longest day, 21 June. It is these freaks of nature that make the English climate so interesting.

If St Swithun's weeps the weather will be foul for forty days.

This is a doubtful forecast; it has been proved that a wet St Swithun's (15 July) more often than not results in a fine summer.

The number forty is very prominent in weather proverbs, and is also significant in the Bible. For forty days the rain fell while Noah was in the Ark; Moses was forty days on Mount Sinai, Elijah was forty days in the wilderness, Christ was also forty days in the wilderness.

We had sixteen weeks' frost in February.

After the hard winter of 1947 I commented to our old worker Jim what a hard winter we had had and such a lot of snow. Jim replied, 'You don't remember 1898 I suppose. That was the winter we had sixteen weeks frost in February.' I thought to myself that the

The Green, Northleach

Returning from the fields to Hampnett village with the horse teams at the end of the day, 1935

February of 1898 was a long one, and then Jim added, 'We had a lovely spring because I remember that your Uncle George and me were hoeing the wheat in March.'

The owls that mark the setting sun declare
A starlight night and a morning fair.

The one thing that usually forecasts a fine day is the hooting of the Tawny Owl. I have listened to its call in the winter when we have been visiting the rabbit snares on the hill and the promise of a 'starlight night and a morning fair' has been fulfilled. The Tawny Owl's call does forecast good weather.

Mackerel sky, not long wet, not long dry.

Yes, there is truth in the old rhyme. When the clouds are mottled, a mixture of blue and grey, the weather will be unsettled.

The farther the sight the nearer the rain.

Another couplet. 'The farther the sight the nearer the rain' is disappointing to anyone who has arranged an outing the following day. If one can see a long way it does mean that rain is coming.

Rain before seven fine before eleven.

There is truth in that. A bright morning is often followed by a wet day, but if the early morning is wet one looks to a break in the clouds and better weather in the afternoon.

*When the swallows fly high that is a sign of good
weather and good weather to come.*

This is quite true, and relates to the fact that the insects they feed
on fly higher in fine weather.

The Countryman's Weatherglass.

The Scarlet Pimpernel, a pretty plant, is known as 'The Countryman's Weatherglass' or 'The Shepherd's Weatherglass'. Many a
time when we have been hoeing mangolds in June and the plant
has had to fall to the hoe it has been a picture on a fine day. When
the blossom closes it is a sure sign of rain to come.

*Look up in the sky and when the rooks start
cider-making up there it will rain.*

Some years ago I was called upon to do a little programme on the
radio regarding forecasting of weather. I asked my friend Wilson
what he looked for as a sign of rain. Without hesitating he replied:
'Look up in the sky and when the rooks start cider-making up there
it will rain.' I said, 'Cider making! What do you mean?' 'Ah!' he
said, 'That's my way of describing how the rooks go round in circles
and do their dive-bombing.' It was a good description after all.

Dr Jenner of Berkeley in Gloucestershire wrote in the nineteenth century:

> And see yon rooks how odd their flight.
> They imitate the gliding kite,
> And seem precipitate to fall,
> As if they felt the piercing ball.
> Twill surely rain. I see with sorrow
> Our jaunt must be put off tomorrow.

The Oak before the Ash we shall only get a splash.
The Ash before the Oak we shall surely get a soak.

One saying which was commonplace among the folk on the land but which was surely a fallacy. This jingle referred to the Oak leaf being on the tree before the Ash leaf and supposedly thus forecasting a good summer. I have watched the leafing of Oak and Ash trees all my life. Never have I seen the Ash in leaf before the Oak; the Ash is well known to be late in putting forth its leaves.

When Bredon Hill puts on its cap
men of the Vale beware of that.

This is a saying from the Star at Ashton-under-Hill, where the old men were weather-wise. Bredon Hill was their weather forecaster. The Vale of Evesham looks towards the hill and Bredon's cap – that is, a mist shrouding the top of the hill – is a sure sign of rain.

CHAPTER TWO

Planting the Land

It has always fascinated me the way the old farmers and market gardeners put so much stay on dates in the calendar. We know that calendars used to have red-letter days and the dates of fairs and saints' days shown in red. In planting and harvesting crops our ancestors relied on these special days.

Why did the countryman plant his early potatoes on Good Friday? Good Friday, as we know, is a movable celebration. At the turn of the century farmers and landlords insisted that their men went to church on Good Friday morning and they then had the afternoon as a holiday. This gave them the opportunity to plant their early potatoes.

When the Elm leaf is as big as a penny
You will have to plant if you are going to have any.

Runner bean planting was judged not by the calendar but by how early the Elm tree came into leaf. The complete saying is: 'When the Elm leaf is as big as a farthing it's time to plant runner beans in the garden. When the Elm leaf is as big as a penny you will have to plant if you are going to have any.' It is very good advice, but what a pity that so many Elm trees are no longer with us.

Spring is when you can put your foot on three daisies.

I would not bank on this one, for sometimes daisies grow all winter but they do of course multiply in the spring when the land warms.

Gardeners used to sit bare-backed on the land to test the temperature before they planted their seeds. If it was too cold to sit down they delayed planting!

The crops and the seasons are thirteen months behind those in the Vale.

Up on the Cotswold Hills where my old friend Frank Court used to tell me this, with a smile, they would never plant runner beans until Stow Fair Day, 12 May. His uncle, who I knew very well, and who worked as a bailiff on a farm near the River Avon, used to plant runner beans on 17 March and was always first on the market. The land next to the river did not take the frost. It is a scientific fact that the land by water is free from spring frosts. We planted runner beans 600 feet up on Bredon Hill. The spring frosts did not reach up there! We planted on 17 March too, but the beans were not up so early on the bleak hill.

Sow four grains in a row.
One for the pigeon,
One for the crow,
One to rot and another to grow.

Rooks will not take runner beans from the rows where they are planted, but they will steal broad beans, horse beans and peas just after they emerge from the ground. In 1934 our runner beans were planted in a newly-ploughed pasture field. Under turf wireworms are plentiful, often one million to an acre. The wireworms attacked the runner bean seed under the ground, and the rooks, which are partial to wireworms, dug up the beans to get at the worms. These birds were really doing a good job in getting rid of a pest but we had to replant the field with runner beans and keep the rooks away.

In 1942 I planted 5 acres of Brussels sprouts in a field which had been a pasture the year before. In 5 acres of sprouts there are 25,000 plants. The plants had taken root and were growing well, but when I visited the field a few days later on Whit Monday the rooks had pulled up almost all of the plants to get at the wireworms!

The idea behind this old saying is that it was necessary to plant four seeds in order to get one plant. Planting and how one plants the seed and how much is planted per acre depends on soil conditions and on the time of the year. More wheat seed has to be drilled per acre in the spring than in the autumn. The autumn wheat tillers bush-like while the spring wheat goes ahead without a check.

Some crops have to be thinned or singled. In the past this was done with a hoe, nowadays the farmer uses a precision drill which plants the seed at intervals. So many summer days have I spent with Tom, the cowman, singling mangolds. George and I planted the mangold seed in April, Red Chiefs and Golden Tankards. When the crop came up we hoed between the rows and then two weeks later we singled the roots, leaving a space of about 10 inches between the plants. We used hoes with a 7-inch plate to single the plants.

The best manure is the farmer's foot.

Many's the time the land is neglected when the farmer fails to survey his land. By studying the soil for moisture a farmer knows when to plant. By rubbing the ears of corn in his hand he knows when the wheat is fit to harvest. The man who charges round his farm in a Land Rover instead of walking does not really discover the needs of crops or livestock.

Dress seed wheat with vitriol and make the sign of the cross.

One of the diseases of wheat is called Stinking Smut. It is something which attacks the ears of the wheat and greatly reduces the yield. Today seed wheat is dressed with a mercurial powder to prevent Smut. Many years ago we dressed seed wheat in a very different way, with vitriol. The seed was put on the stone floor of the barn, and some vitriol mixed into a solution with water was sprinkled on it. Then we turned it with shovels until every grain had been dressed with the mixture. This was left overnight to dry ready for planting the following day. Our cowman then took a rick peg and put a cross with the peg on the heap of wheat. 'What's that for?' I asked him. 'Oh,' he replied, 'we have always put the sign of the cross on the seed. That's to protect the seed from the Devil. You can't be too careful. It's a good protection.'

As hollow as a Puck Fice.

Here's a saying from Shepherd Tidmarsh, it refers to the land.

A Puck Fice is a Cotswold name for the puff ball toadstool, which sends showers of fine particles into the air when picked. This Cotswold shepherd, Tidmarsh, was speaking as a Shakespearean when he called a Puff Ball a Puck Fice. The fairy rings where the toadstools grow were known as Puck Rings; Puck speaks of mischief. To describe the land as being 'as hollow as a Puck Fice' is a good description. Certain crops need firm soil, wheat in particular.

During the war when we had to plough up the pastures, one of the difficulties was getting the soil firm enough after the turf had been turned over. Hollow land is a good harbour for wireworms and ploughed up pasture had a large population of these pests which feed on the roots of young wheat plants. We rolled the land with heavy rollers but still had a lot of wireworm damage. Where the tractor turned on the headland the soil was compacted and here the wheat grew unmolested. We do not see wheat rolled so much today. The heavy Cambridge roller in the spring breaks the clods and gives the soil a good tilth.

—————

The land is like a woman. When it needs squeezing it needs squeezing tight.

Here is good common sense regarding the land, I do not know about women!

When the land was rolled by the two or three horses pulling a Cambridge or Ring Roll the horses moved at about 3 miles per hour, a steady pace. Modern tractors can be quite fast. It is easy to understand that if the roller is pulled too fast by the tractor it does very little good.

I remember our cowman watching a young tractor driver going, as he said, 'Hell for leather' with a roller over a wheat field. 'He's doing no good,' the cowman said, 'the roller barely touches the ground. He's just wasting the Gaffer's time and the tractor fuel.'

CHAPTER THREE

The Church

That field is as full of squitch as Hell's full of Parsons.

The carter used an expression in those early days that I have never heard before nor since if a field was particularly foul with weeds, couch grass (squitch) in particular.

Did the farmworker of the 1920s think this about the parson? Our carter used to say that parsons in general were very passionate! I asked him why and he said, 'It's because they don't have to work like thee and me. They be the worst.' I replied, 'Ah, but the parson who has just passed our team in his Governess car has got a housekeeper who plays the organ in church.' The man with the four-horse team coming in with me at the end of the day said, 'Housekeeper? That's what you call her. You mean a lie by 'cause if there was a fire they would both come out of the same bedroom window!'

God loves the Crow as well as he loves the Nightingale.

He sings like a Bumble Bee in a churn.

Many years ago at the village chapel a local preacher also sang a solo. I said to one of the older members that the solo was not all that tuneful. He replied, 'God loves the Crow as well as he loves the Nightingale.'

That dog's as sensible as a Christian.

I've heard this said about a dog that is well-trained and obedient.

———

As sure as God's in Gloucestershire.

A common saying which derives from the fact that there are more churches in Gloucestershire than in most other counties. The churches were built from the income received from the wool trade in the Middle Ages. Churches like Chipping Campden and Northleach are known as Wool Churches.

———

God tempers the wind to the shorn lamb.

We like to think that our problems and troubles are not more than we can bear. The shorn lamb does not like the east wind. We like to think that God shelters us from some of the worst things in life.

———

God made the country, man made the town.

This seems a bit strong, yet some developments have marred the earthly scene, other buildings have complemented nature.

———

'Battering the gates of Heaven with storms of prayer.'

These words of Tennyson's are so true. I have heard the storms of prayer and think that a few seasonable words would have been better.

Northleach Congregational Chapel, Gloucestershire, 1903

Bellringers

A villager repairing a cane chair seat outside her cottage

Family prayers are nearly a thing of the past. A friend of mine said to me one day: 'Before we have breakfast Father has to give God his orders for the day.'

I am in favour of simplicity rather than long-winded pontifications.

Better that you had never been born
Than to have your hair cut on a Sunday morn.

Sunday observance as practised by the Puritans survived into the Victorian age. This and the following saying are just two of the many sayings which reveal the inhibitions of the Victorians so evident in the country when I was a boy.

Regarding Sunday haircutting, I remember a chap known as Harry Fly by Night cutting farmworkers' hair on Sunday mornings. Harry was a great character in the village, a bellringer who became captain of the bellringers. When they were ringing, his call of 'Next time' for the ringers to follow with his bell was one way of him keeping the change ringing in sequence.

Harry had a kitchen chair in the garden where he practised his art with the scissors. The men waiting their turn on summer Sunday mornings sat on hampers. The great attraction of having a hair cut from Harry was his home-made wine which his customers sampled. One chap named Percy used to faint when he had his hair cut. Harry used to revive him with a drop of brandy. Percy's fainting was somewhat put on! After the last man had had his hair cut the villagers went round the garden, looked at his large marrows, prodded his pig and estimated its weight. A Sunday social occasion.

A Sunday well spent brings a week of content.

Strict observation of the Sabbath was seen well into the early part of this century. One man was so particular that he used to give his pigs enough food on Saturday so that he did not need to feed them on Sunday. His two sons were expected to clean his boots on Saturday in readiness for him to go to church the following day. One Saturday they forgot to clean them. On Sunday morning the boys were cleaning their father's boots when their father came into the kitchen. 'Stop!' he cried, and the boys put the boots down. 'I'm not having my boots cleaned on a Sunday,' he said. One boot had been cleaned and polished and the other had not. He went to church with one dirty boot and one clean one!

The better the day the better the deed.

This is a contradictory saying, a sort of licence for working on a Sunday. A market gardener I knew said when he commented on folks working on a Sunday, 'I'm not too keen on working in the week let alone on Sunday!'

Ladies: Oh for a man, Oh for a man, Oh for a
mansion in the skies.

Men: Lord send Sal, Lord send Sal, Lord send
Salvation to our hearts.

The lines of this anthem were commonly voiced and it is a sure thing that the division of words had a humorous effect on the congregation.

There has been much unconscious humour in the Nonconformist churches and chapels. It is undoubtedly because they are run by laity. A local preacher announced the preacher for the following Sunday. It was to be Hugh Price-Hughes, MA. He announced the man as the spelling read: 'Hug Price-Hugs Ma.'

A great deal of emphasis was given by the old preachers to

Temperance, the Band of Hope in particular, where they sang:

> I like with a friend an hour to pass.
> I'm very fond of a social glass,
> But it must be filled with water.
> Water pure doth brighter shine
> Than Brandy, Gin or Sparkling Wine.
> Sad is the fix if the Liquor you mix,
> You never do that nor I, nor I.
> You never do that nor I.

If a woman who has had a baby enters someone's house before going to church to thank God for the safe arrival of her baby, there will be a baby born in that house in less than a year's time.

This idea was prevalent when I was a boy and mothers were churched after their baby was born. There is, of course, a service in the Prayer Book called 'The Churching of Women'.

Not so many years ago a relative of mine took her baby into a neighbour's house before she had been to church and in 'The Churching of Women' service thanked God for the safe delivery of her baby. The woman in the neighbour's house had an unmarried daughter going steady with a market gardener. She said quite openly after my relative had gone, 'I didn't thank her for coming into my house before she had been churched, especially as our Mary is not married and going steady with Albert.' I reckoned she would keep an eye on Mary until the year was over!

CHAPTER FOUR

About Fruit

*If apples bloom in March in vain for them you'll
search.
If apples bloom in April well then they will be
plentiful.
If apples bloom in May you may eat them night and
day.*

This proverb relates to spring frosts. When we grew apples and
plums the growers always lived in fear when there was a March
blossom. Not only the frosts but the cold winds would kill the
flower. It was such a long while to wait from March until the
blossom was safe in May. Sometimes frosts thin out the blossom
and that is a good thing, especially with Victoria Plums. There is
nothing worse than a thick crop of Victorias.

Evesham market gardeners were very pessimistic when a frost
came late in the spring. 'It's killed the lot' and 'It was sharp enough
last night to kill the hovels!' are comments I have heard many
times and yet when the plums and apples were ready to pick half a
crop was left and the price was good.

Some gardeners lit fires under their trees when frost was
imminent. Raymond Bush, a horticulturalist, made a study of
spring frosts and what is known as 'frost pockets' where the
frost lies and kills blossom. He it was who advized a local estate
where to plant their fruit trees on the south-west slopes of
Bredon Hill, and what lovely fruit they grew up there in the
1930s and 40s!

Michaelmas and a little before half the apple's thrown away with the core.
Christmas and a little bit after if it's as sour as a crab it's 'Thank you, Master.'

This saying speaks for itself. At Michaelmas there is so much fruit around and the varieties of apples are legion, from Beauty of Bath to Worcester Pearmain.

In a good year many apples are wasted. The early varieties do not keep and are best eaten straight from the tree. As the year progresses the number of varieties which can be stored diminishes. The early cookers, like Warners King or Drunken Willy, will have gone yellow in the straw where they have been stored. Even the Blenheim Orange is at its best before Christmas. The favourite keeping apples were the ones which the old folk said would keep until apples come again.

When foreign apples first came into the country in the spring they were looked upon with suspicion. The first foreign apple I tasted was when I was in my teens.

During the Second World War English apples were relished. Regardless of flavour, any apple which was a certain size could be sold at a fixed price. Since then there has been a great increase in the growing of Cox's Orange. It is the best apple, an English Cox! Cheaper Golden Delicious from the continent bear no comparison in my opinion.

When the apple is ripe it will fall.

The saying comes from our cowman Tom. He was more than a cowman. I considered him to be a cow doctor! He had an eye for anything amiss in animals. As a boy I stood with Tom in the barn waiting for a cow to calve. We watched by the light of a hurricane lantern. Tom had noticed during the day that Ada, the deep red

Shorthorn, had what he called 'bagged up'. The teats of her udder were waxy. She showed shape, as it was called, had swollen, and she twitched her tail. Ada went down on a straw bed and heaved.

'Shall we help her?' I asked Tom.

'No,' he replied. 'When the apple's ripe it will fall.'

At midnight Ada had a lovely heifer calf.

Till St Swithun's Day be past
The apples are not fit to taste.

As sure as God made little apples.

There could never be anything more sure than that when the blossom falls some little apples will appear. St Swithun's Day, 15 July, is known in the country as Apple Christening Day. The story of St Swithun, the Winchester Saint is interesting. Forty days wet or dry, yet 15 July is a good day for apple christening. When I was a boy we looked forward to Apple Christening Day and never ate an apple until then.

On the one tree of Beauty of Bath the fruit had been colouring for the past weeks. On 15 July we sampled the apples. They were still a bit sharp but they were the first apples of the season. Foreign apples there may have been but we did not see any of those. The Beauty of Bath, christened or not, made 15 July a red letter day on the calendar.

An apple a day keeps the doctor away.

Apples no doubt are very healthy fruit to eat. It is recognized that they are preferable to citrus fruit from abroad.

The end of the rhyme about apples goes: 'An onion a day keeps anybody away!' Onions too are a good food.

Lifting potatoes

Market gardeners in the Vale of Evesham

Mr Martin, the first man to grow purple *Pershore plums*

Everything in the garden is lovely except the rhubarb and that's gone to seed.

This humorous fable is very old. Rhubarb is always spoken of in a family lightheartedly. It comes up year by year, provides pies and jam and wine and then goes to seed. It is a spring plant and is not recommended as food after July.

The words are really another way of saying 'everything is hunky-dory' or 'everything is OK'.

This idea about rhubarb may also stem from its cultivation in cottage gardens. In the days before indoor sanitation rhubarb was fertilized from the privy. I remember complimenting Jim, who worked for me, on the excellence of the rhubarb he gave me, only to hear from him: 'I'll tell you how it grows so well. We allus empties the closet bucket on it.'

As sour as Varges.

I recall my Dad describing fruit in this way. Varges was verjuice, the juice of sour grapes, which was used as a medicine for cattle and horses.

> Be sure of Varges, a gallon at least.
> So good for the kitchen, so needful for beast.
> It helpeth the cattle so feeble and faint,
> If timely such cattle with it thou acquaint.

Verjuice was given, a pint at a time, to treat cattle with a disease called flux. This, I believe, is a condition with which a beast loses its cud and stops ruminating. When this occurred on our farm, Dad's partner used to boil some fat bacon in cabbage water and use it as a drench. I would think that medicine would bring anything back up.

At Michaelmas the Devil walks and spits on the blackberries.

Blackberries it is true are better before Michaelmas, by 29 September we often get frosts and these frosts make the berries musky. Our ancestors blamed the Devil for this, that figures!

You ask me where and when I come
From Pershore where d'ye think?
Where do we grow the yellow plums?
Why Pershore where d'ye think?
Hop gatherers jest in ribald vein
O'er clustering hops they pull,
While farmers reap the golden grain
And pack the granaries full.
But we content in merriment
Will let the glasses clink.
For all is peace and plenty
At Pershore where d'ye think.

You ask me where and whence I come.
From Pershore, God help us.
Don't ask about the crops at home. God help us
Last April every sprig and spray
Was decked with pearly blossoms gay.
Last August every branch and bough
Was bent with yellow plums, but now,
God help us.

These two rhymes from Pershore in Hereford and Worcester speak for themselves. The plum crop has been vital in the past for the fruit growers of Pershore. When the spring frosts killed the blossom it was a tragedy. It was then that the growers would plant vegetable marrows for the jam factory because there would be a shortage of plums for jam, the marrows being a substitute for the yellow egg plums. Of course, in a good season things were much brighter for the growers.

When the plum blossom was killed by frost some of the smallholders would congregate and drink themselves silly on home-made wine. I have heard it said when the crop was a failure, 'They'll be pulling the smallholders out of the river.' Men have drowned themselves, feeling poverty stricken and hopeless.

A man named Crook discovered the first Pershore Plum tree growing in Tydlessly Wood. It is different from many varieties. It grows true from a stock, thus it needs no grafting. It does make excellent jam.

CHAPTER FIVE

Bulls, Cows and Calves

He doesn't know A from a Bull's foot.

This common Gloucestershire saying speaks for itself but I wonder what the connection is between A and a Bull's Foot. A bull's feet do tend to grow when he is tied up and not having much exercise. We used to trim the feet of our Hereford bull. Herefords are generally docile and these days are kept in the field with the cows.

The bull has the advantage over the A.I. operator. During the winter when the nights are dark and long it is quite often that a cow will come on bulling after dark and will be gone off by daylight. This is where the bull running with the cows will serve the cow in season.

A neighbour of mine had his cow served with A.I. He told me about it and remarked that he did not think that the cow had enjoyed it very much. When my cows were first served by the A.I. man he said that the glass tube which he used to inject the serum was longer than the bull's penis. My old cowman argued with him and said 'I know that a bull's tool is longer than your tube.' I was amused.

He doesn't care whether the cow calves or the bull breaks his neck.

This was a common criticism of us young farmworkers in the village, and was said in a jocular way by Mr Bailey about me. He was Dad's partner and I got on very well with him. When I was sixteen what he said about me was perfectly true. I had a good home, and life among the crops and stock on the farm was fascinating to me. I was looking after a suckling herd of cows and rearing calves. The bull stood in a pen over Mr Bailey's garden wall. That year the water supply dried up in the bull pen and I had to carry water from Mr Bailey's house. Sometimes Joker, our bull, did not get as much water as he could drink.

I suppose the manner of my dress prompted the remark. In those days I wore breeches and puttees, and an old grey jacket with a poacher's pocket which came in handy when I was out with Mr Bailey and he shot what we called a 'long tailed un', a pheasant. Dad agreed with his partner's assessment of me and said he thought I ought to train for a parson as I did not care what people said about me!

A bull should not only be a good sort but also a good sort of bull.

Choosing a bull to use on a dairy herd is one thing, the milk record of its dam is important, while with a beef bull there is much more emphasis on conformation. We liked a Hereford bull that was not too leggy, 'Not too much daylight under him!' our cowman would say. A bull with good hindquarters so that the calves he sires have more roasting joints in their carcass than boiling joints. I once reared some calves I had bought which were half-bred Hereford/Ayrshire crosses. They looked all right as calves but when they were two-years-old they had pointed instead of square rumps. Not the fault of the bull, he was a good sort of bull – he had a good pedigree.

Our neighbour had a white Shorthorn bull. The theory was that if a white Shorthorn bull served a red Shorthorn cow she would produce a roan calf. Roan heifers were desirable. We took some of our cows to the white bull, our cows being red Shorthorns, and they had roan calves. The mystery was that our neighbour did not have such luck. His red Shorthorns had some red calves and some white ones.

Half the pedigree goes in at the mouth.

It is true, proper feeding is important, but obviously however good the feeding that will not compensate for a badly bred animal. If the breeding is there, even if the beast is not looked after and fed well, the proper farming of the animal will obtain results.

When I was farming and in the local market one day in April a bunch of poor, thin cattle came into the ring. I knew the farm where they came from and that they had had a bad winter as outliers on the hill and been fed a supplement of only a little oat straw. The cattle haulier had taken them to market early in the day but they were to be offered at the end of the sale. They looked thin and hungry but were cross-bred Old Gloucesters by a Hereford bull. An old farmer friend said to me, 'Are you looking for some store cattle? This bunch will do you, all they need is some good keep.' I said, 'Do you think they will live?' Harry replied, 'They will come cheap. You and me know the farm.' The bidding started low, possibly by the auctioneer. I bid £26, and they were standing at £27 and I hesitated. 'Go on, Fred. Have another bid,' my friend said. I bought them for £28 per head.

On my pasture at home when I went to count them in the mornings the animals worried me. After a hungry winter the spring grass had purged them. I went to see my friend Harry. He said: 'Give them some cotton cake. That will bind them!' They had refused good hay because there was plenty of grass in the meadow. I gave them cotton cake and after a few weeks they lost their rough winter coats and looked a picture.

I sold them in November at £74 per head, probably the best deal I ever had, thanks to Harry.

A milking scene in Sussex, from a postcard franked Ramsgate 28 May 1907

The butcher's boy

Bill Spires holding a twenty-one hundredweight bull named Samson in 1915

Market day at Moreton-in-Marsh, c. 1906

Cows have five mouths.

If the weather is wet cows poach the land. They have what is known as five mouths, one to eat the grass and their four feet to tread it into the ground. It is interesting to note that in old tenancy agreements landlords stipulated that some fields, good feeding pastures, should not be stocked with milking cows.

A gallon of milk from the cow is worth two from the bucket.

Nature's way of calf rearing is, obviously, for the cow to give all her milk to the new-born calf. With high-yielding cows that are kept expressly for milk production the calf is reared artificially on milk substitute. Of course calves thrive that way, being bucket fed.

I used to rear three calves on a newly calved cow, her own calf and two from the market. Some cows will let any calf suckle, others will kick and be difficult. The most important thing is that when the calves are suckled twice a day the cow's own calf suckles on the inside next to her mother. So two calves suckle on one side and one on the other.

When the calves were weaned at three months old the system was to put two fresh calves on the cow. By then she was quite happy to let all three of the first lot have her milk. When the two young calves were put to her she had difficulty in accepting them. More problems could arise when those two were weaned and she was given one new calf to finish her lactation.

Of course it is therapeutic for calves to suck rather than to drink from a bucket. Single suckling of calves produces wonderful offspring. When the calves were born out in the fields in March and stayed there until November they took all their mother's milk and rarely suffered from calf scour because the colostrum, or what we called beastings or cherry curds, gave them immunity from such ills; they also grew lovely thick coats to protect them from the weather. Single sucklers, called 'lug tits', made good prices at the autumn sales.

An in-calf cow is one that has been to a whist drive.

Got by a porter out of a railway van.

She was married late in life.

These frivolous auctioneers' sayings I remember hearing as a boy, when the auctioneer was such a wag. I listened to his banter, which now could be described as 'The Wisdom of the Ancients'.

The reference to whist drives reminds me of a time many years ago when a lady started some whist drives and dances for the young folk of the village. The old-fashioned father of one of the village girls declared 'I shan't let our Mary go to the whist drives and dances because I know what happens and there will soon be some bastard kids in the village.' Mary did not go, but she was the only girl to give birth to what I prefer to call a 'love child'!

The saying 'Got by a porter out of a railway van' referred to a rather weakly-looking Jersey calf which had no pedigree. The dealers do like to try it on with auctioneers, this man was up to their tricks.

The third saying was the auctioneer's reply when a very old cow with a crumpled horn came into the ring. She was catalogued as a heifer and her calf. One dealer looked at her teeth and the rings on her horns and said, 'This is no heifer. It's an old cow.' The auctioneer replied, 'My instructions are to sell her as a heifer and her calf and all I can say is that she must have been married very late in life.'

If you deal in calves you will be a calf all your life.

This old saying may sound rather odd, for some calf dealers have done very well for themselves and certainly have not remained as calves or little men.

To me the saying does have some truth in it. It is all about speculation. I knew a farmer named Frank. He farmed 250 acres, and in what are sometimes called 'the hungry thirties' wheat growing did not pay, so he became a market gardener. Frank refused to go under or become 'a calf'. He grew many acres of peas and some broad beans. The peas picked in rotation usually paid him, broad beans were more difficult. The market was very uncertain: some years the beans sold well, other years they were unsaleable. Frank told me always to follow a bad year by planting a few extra acres. Some get downhearted and do not plant any. With a fairly big acreage, Frank told me: 'If the beans sell you make a lot of money, if you plant a few very little. I said, 'If there is no sale for beans and you have planted a lot, you lose a lot.' Frank was a cute grower, he replied, 'It's swings and round-abouts.' He was one man who did not remain a calf all his life.

More rain more rest.
More rain more grass for the cow, sir.

The first line of this saying is a very old one recited by plough boys on a wet day. In the old days the carter and his plough boy would often clean and mend harness on wet days. Sometimes they would be chaff cutting in the barn.

If a boy said 'More rain more rest' in the ear-shot of the farmer and the farmer asked him, 'What did you say, my boy?', the boy's reply would be: 'More rain more grass for the cow, sir.'

CHAPTER SIX

Health and Ailments

A hot cross bun baked on Good Friday when kept for a year is good medicine to give to a child with the belly ache.

I heard this saying from my Uncle George and he declared it to be true. He told me of families where hot cross buns baked on Good Friday were kept in the chimney corner for giving to children with stomach upsets. Perhaps the growth of the mould of penicillin on the buns acted as an antibiotic.

Uncle George held many standard superstitions but he looked upon bread as something sacred. Bread was never to be wasted. If, when I was a boy, we wasted bread at bait time (our ten o'clock 'lunch') he would warn us that one day we would go hungry. To burn a bit of crust was criminal, although he did feed the birds in his garden with scraps of bread.

Neglect your belly and you're soon on your back.

This may be true in some cases, but to live too well is bad also.

During the 1939 war when rationing was so strict, folk were healthier. My old workman, Jim, who had worked on a coal round before he came to me in his seventies was lean and fit. He lived very frugally, bread and dripping for lunch, and the dripping had to be imagined, it was so thin. He lived to be over ninety.

During the war most of us in the country kept a pig. It was a stand-by. Our stockman fed a good pig and he had it killed in

Mrs Betty Smith, district nurse at Colesbourne, c. 1908–10

An old gentleman standing outside Arlington Row, Bibury in the Cotswolds

March. He enjoyed the bacon. His wife said to him one day, 'When are we going to start the hams?' Tom replied, 'We are going to eat the ham when "young Fred" (that was me) wants some long hours put in haymaking.' In the hay field it was good to see him with ham instead of margarine between his bread.

————

If you'd live to be old, strip before you sweat and dress before you are cold.

A saying from the Gloucestershire/Warwickshire border, and good advice.

————

A creaking gate hangs a long time.

We have all experienced a creaking farm gate. Some said that the reason they creaked was that they were hung badly. 'I don't know whether this gate was hung or drowned,' was a note of sarcasm cast at the farm handyman. Gates do creak, just as inn signs creak in the wind if they are not oiled.

The estate adjoining my farm took a pride in their gates. Every one had the date when it was made in the estate yard stamped upon it. The landowner at the time was a hunting man and point-to-point rider. He kept a good lot of horses and once broke his collar bone riding in the Grand National at Becher's Brook. On his land on the hill there were lots of hunting gates with a spring fastener. If the gentlemen of the hunt could not open one with a riding crop they reported it to the estate office and someone had to rectify it *at once* – not the next day! I do not think there were any creaking gates on his land.

The expression is often applied to people, and it is so true. We meet folk in every walk of life who are always ailing. Some suffer without complaint, but others appear to enjoy being ill. They quote what the doctor said. They take pills for this and pills for that but, as the saying goes, they hang on a long time. Appearances are so deceptive, a healthy looking person can die young, and an ailing person can yet live to old age.

He's seen too many Christmas Days.

This is an old saying that folk who are old and infirm use as a reason for not being able to do what they once could.

As a young man my uncle could carry a sack of wheat thinking nothing of it. He would carry it up steps without any problem. When he grew old, he confided in me and said, 'I used to be able to carry a sack of wheat, 2 cwt 28 lb, now it takes me all my strength to carry an empty sack.'

Some country folk are quite philosophical about old age and even impending death.

I don't think he will need many more clean shirts.

I have only heard one man say this; it's an original. What a way to describe someone who looks on the way out, as it is said!

The man who coined this saying was referring to someone we both knew. He was a difficult man and when it was said I wondered whether it was wishful thinking. However the man lived for many more years, a creaking gate.

CHAPTER SEVEN

Concerning Sheep

All goes to the Devil when the shepherd is evil.

There is no doubt that shepherds on the farm are a race apart from the other workers. It is a skilled job and a good farmer will respect his shepherd and treat him accordingly. The farmer will not order his shepherd, 'You do this tomorrow.' He will say: 'Do you think, Shepherd, that it's advisable to drench the lambs?' The shepherd in charge of his flock is depended upon to do the right thing at the right time.

I have never met an evil shepherd but I remember one chap on a neighbouring farm we called a 'galloping shepherd'! He was always on the run; his flock was never a thriving one. A shepherd should take his time with his sheep, spend ten minutes leaning on the field gate and observing. It is then that the little ills which befall sheep can be discovered.

Shepherd Tidmarsh told me that he knew of a shepherd who had been sacked by his employer and bore a grudge. He did a slight operation on the rams at tupping time which made the rams infertile so that the ewes were not in lamb. Here was an example of 'All goes to the Devil when the shepherd is evil.' Other shepherds have choked a lamb with a ball of wool so that they could say they had found the lamb dead and share the meat with the farmer.

I am sure that the majority of shepherds have been devoted to their flocks. Our Shepherd Tidmarsh was a past master at the art of shepherding. He rarely made a mistake. The day the lambs were tailed, the shepherd needed help and he got it. It was he who said which of the men he needed and he got that man. If the ewes needed mangolds the carter had to keep a load in the field where the lambing ewes were in the early spring. The farmer saw that the shepherd was never short of mangolds; the best hay and clover was for the lambing ewes. In fact, Shepherd Tidmarsh insisted that his ewes had Sainfoin hay from the hill brought down on a farm wagon and put in the lambing pens. When the carter and boy fetched the Sainfoin they were instructed that any of the mouldy fodder from the top of the rick or from the staddle was not to go on the wagon.

During the night at lambing time Alf Tidmarsh stayed with the ewes in the thatched barn. Dad used to relieve him for four hours in the evening from six o'clock until ten. It was as if the sheep belonged to the shepherd. When the flock was struck by liver fluke in the 1920s he threatened to drown himself in the moat pond. He told me, 'I don't mind carrying any tool around the farm except the spade.' He had just buried four ewes.

A sheep's biggest enemy is another sheep.

Farm land can get what is known as 'sheep sick'. What it really means is that sheep have been kept continually on the land for many years. Land farmed in this way results in a build up of diseases and parasites, such as worms and fluke. If a sheep farmer moves his flock to a farm where sheep have not been kept he will have very little trouble from diseases the first year.

Lowland farms adjoining streams and with stagnant ponds are a harbour for the Fluke Snail. The history of the Fluke Snail is an interesting one, but the snail has brought devastation to the sheep farmer in the past. Apparently, the year 1879 was a disaster for sheep farmers. They lost most of their sheep in that very wet year with liver fluke. Veterinary scientists have now developed drugs and injections to combat this menace.

In the 1920s liver fluke was still prevalent. I remember Dad buying some Oxford ewes from Stratford-upon-Avon. We lost a lot of the animals until we dosed them with carbon tetrachloride.

Every time a ewe died the shepherd said to Dad, 'It's one of those you bought from Stratford, Master.' Dad had only bought twenty and he told the shepherd, 'I should think by now all the Stratford ewes are dead.' The shepherd replied, 'I never liked them yows and noticed one or two with glassy eyes and lumpy jaws. When that happens it's all over.'

Lambs born on farms which are sheep sick are liable to get lamb dysentery and pulpy kidney disease. The new-born lambs pick up these ailments through their naval. Nowadays the new-born lamb can be immunized soon after birth. When I took over the shepherding on my father's farm from Shepherd Tidmarsh in the 1930s the old thatched Cross Barn in the village had been the maternity unit for the sheep as long as anyone could remember. The shepherd had the barn divided into little hurdled private pens to house the ewe and her new-born lamb until they went out into the adjoining orchard. A corral outside the barn enclosed the in-lamb ewes. After the ewes lambed that first year a lot of the lambs went down with what turned out to be lamb dysentery. They had diarrhoea! I bought the medicine for it but, of course, the lambs were already infected and quite a lot died. I concluded that the problem was in an infection picked up by the lambs through their navels being in contact with the infected floor of the barn. The next year I moved the flock into another barn and had very little trouble.

Of course, the healthiest place for a ewe to lamb is out in the field or on the hill. It is fascinating how a ewe will find a particular spot to lamb. She may circle the field in labour for a time while she chooses the spot to have her lamb. The saying 'As silly as a sheep' is simply not true.

Never let a sheep hear the church bells twice in the same field.

This leads on from the previous saying. Sheep thrive best of all when they are moved from one field to another. I found when I took over the flock from Alf Tidmarsh that the sheep thrived on 'pastures new'.

The shepherd had continued to work with the flock when he was old and infirm. He had kept the sheep near the farm buildings close to the village. The fields highest on the hill had not been grazed by sheep for years. I took them up there and we had some bonny lambs.

A sheep's fart is better than a cow's turd.

This saying came from a very good farmer who farmed before my time. He only had one arm, having lost the other on a mechanical chaff-cutter or mangel-pulper. His observation is quite true, sheep do improve the pasture land. When they are fed on corn and cake their dung does wonders with the herbage. I knew a farmer who farmed some hill land which was poor. He was a tenant on an estate. The landlord was anxious to improve his land and, concentrates such as linseed cake and cotton cake being cheap at the beginning of this century, he paid for a railway truck load of cake for the sheep, knowing that they would improve the land. This contrasts with the idea that when pasturing milking cows all the goodness from the grass goes into the milk and, as our cowman used to say, 'There's no goodness in a green grass turd from milking cows.'

A ewe full of life is better than one full of teeth.

When I worked with the shepherd we culled the ewes every autumn before we put the tup out. That would be about Michaelmas time. I caught the ewes with the shepherd's crook after we had put them in a hurdled pen. Every ewe was what we called mouthed, its teeth were examined thoroughly. The young-est ewes had two teeth, they were known as theaves. Those a year older had four teeth, these were double theaves. The next year they were called six-tooth ewes and the following year they had eight teeth and were what we called full-mouthed ewes. Some ewes would keep those eight teeth for a few years and if they did they were called 'long in the tooth' because the teeth would grow and become long. Some ewes would lose a tooth soon after they had become full-mouthed, these would be termed 'broken mouthed'.

As I held the ewes for the shepherd he examined each animal very carefully. In the pen by my side I had a paint pot filled with raddle. The shepherd had mixed this marking paste that morning. He had put some raddle powder in the pot and made it into a paste by adding linseed oil. Raddle powder is an oxide of iron and is dark red in colour. If the shepherd found that the ewe he mouthed had two teeth and was therefore a theave, or young ewe, he would say to me, 'Mark that one at the back of her head.' I would dip a short flat stick into the raddle and put a little of the paste on the back of the ewe's head. If the ewe had four teeth I would mark her on the neck, a six-tooth ewe was marked between the shoulders, a full-mouthed ewe was marked in the middle of the back. In this way we could see at a glance the age of the sheep.

A broken-mouthed ewe would be rejected for breeding and the shepherd would say, 'Mark that one on the rump, Fred.' The broken mouthed ewes would go to market, sometimes for slaughter, but some farmers bought broken-mouthed ewes and bred from them for another year. 'A ewe full of life is better than one full of teeth' is quite a good maxim. If the ewe's udder is correct and she is in good condition, she may still give birth to good lambs.

Of course, the theory is that a broken mouthed ewe cannot feed as well as one with a full mouth. When sheep were folded on turnips the broken mouthed ewe was at a disadvantage. Though in some ways a ewe without teeth can graze better than a broken mouthed ewe, especially if the broken mouthed ewe is long in the tooth, some ewes will thrive and rear good lambs when they have no teeth at all. I had one Suffolk ewe which had no teeth for years.

She had twin lambs every year and fed them well. She had no teeth but she was full of milk.

When I was farming I had the misfortune to break a leg one Christmas time. My wife looked after the ewes for a week, then we decided it was best to sell them before they lambed in February. A dealer offered a price for the in-lamb ewes. There were five ewes amongst them which were broken mouthed. The dealer offered a ridiculous price for these so my wife kept them. They had seven lambs between them and fetched a few pounds in the market when they were sold as couples.

I believe the most important thing to watch with ewes is their udders. It is no good lambing a ewe with no milk. Sometimes a ewe will get mastitis in one of her quarters and has only milk in one teat. That is all right if she has a single lamb, but if she has twins one lamb will have to go for adoption. It has always intrigued me that when twin lambs were suckling their mother they always kept to the side which they had begun to suck soon after birth. It is instinct, and once more I must say there is no truth in the saying 'as silly as a sheep'.

'We were as twin lambs that did frisk in the sun and bleat one to the other.'

Shakespeare in *The Winter's Tale* (I, i) paints a picture of spring on the farm and of lambs frisking in the sun.

Opposite the farmhouse where I was born there was an old orchard of gnarled cider apple trees. Orchard grass is not particularly sweet but it comes early in the spring. The ewes and lambs in the orchard were a treat to watch. The lambs would climb on to a fallen log or on to a hillock and then race around the orchard. It was as if one lamb gave the command 'Go' and around they went, stopped for a while and then ran back and frisked in the sun. Sadly, after their tails were cut they never played again. The invention of the elastrator makes this operation bloodless now and the lambs continue to play.

Shepherd Tidmarsh, shepherd for Archer and Bailey from 1916 to 1938, outside Honeysuckle Cottage

Shepherd Tidmarsh with some of his flock on Bredon Hill

Shearing sheep by hand on a Cotswold farm at Eastleach

Shakespeare also says that the lambs 'bleat one to another'. Here is what I believe to be a miracle of nature. When a hundred ewes are in a field with a hundred and fifty lambs each lamb has a different tone when it bleats and is recognized by its mother.

Don't spoil the ship for a ha'porth of tar.

This saying warns against saving a little but losing much, marring a job in order to skimp. Ship, a dialect word, means sheep and the saying refers to the practice of smearing tar on sheep to guard against various infections. This was practised in Shakespeare's day: 'And they [the hands] are often tarred over with the surgery of our sheep.' (From *As You Like It* III, ii.)

This is quite fascinating, because naturally one would think that the tar was used to waterproof a ship. This spelling of sheep as 'ship' is common in the midlands, and inns called The Ship miles from the sea obviously mean The Sheep.

The tar used by the shepherds in Shakespeare's day may have been Stockholm Tar, a healing agent. If a sheep gets struck badly by the blowing fly and the maggots make a raw place on the skin there is nothing better to apply to the wound than Stockholm Tar, the wound heals perfectly.

Two heads are better than one even if they are only sheep's heads.

When a shepherd killed a sheep he was entitled to the offal, the liver and lights, the heart and the head. Two heads, if they are only sheep's heads, obviously will provide more food for the shepherd and his family.

The saying, of course, is also a word in favour of a second opinion. One person with a problem may be flummoxed until another person suggests a way out.

'Of Mastiffs and Mongrels that many we see
A number of thousands too many there be.
Watch therefore in Lent for thy sheep.
Go and look, for dogs will have vitals by Hook or by
Crook.'

Tusser wrote these words in his *Five Hundred Points of Good Husbandry* in the sixteenth century. They are still very true today.

What havoc stray dogs create in a flock of sheep, and their owners do not seem to care. When dogs worry sheep it is usually the work of two animals, a big dog and a little one. They start chasing sheep until an exhausted in-lamb ewe falls and then, if the ewe dies from exhaustion, the dogs feed on the carcase. Otherwise they will kill the ewe. It is not just the sheep that have been attacked that suffer, ewes heavy in lamb will abort if they have been chased.

Some years ago a sheep dog belonging to a neighbouring farmer rounded up my ewes into the corner of a field where there was a deep ditch. The frightened animals fell into the ditch and lay one on top of the other, some died. The guilty dog was a young Collie. The saddest part of this episode was that the dog was doing what he had been trained to do, that is to herd the flock into a corner. When I saw the farmer I found that the young dog was not getting enough work so he took it upon himself to round up my sheep. The farmer paid me for the loss of the sheep and promised to have the dog destroyed. I knew that my neighbour had a lot of sheep on the hill so I asked him whether he had another dog. He told me that he had not. We discussed the problem and I told him that if he promised to keep his dog on a chain except when he was being used to round up his own sheep I would not insist that the dog be put down. When I asked an insurance company to insure my sheep against sheep worrying the application form read as follows: 'Have you had your sheep worried by dogs in the last three years? If so, has the dog been destroyed?' I trusted my neighbour and never filled in the form.

On a previous occasion the farm had been farmed by a hunting man. One Saturday afternoon his two Jack Russell terriers were on my land among my ewes and lambs. I shouted at them and one ran home, the other hung around, so picking him up, I took him home in the Land Rover and locked him in my garage. At six o'clock that evening I rang my neighbour and told him about the dogs. 'Why didn't you put your toe into their ass and send them home?' he said. I replied, 'The one dog is here in the garage. Will you fetch it?' He said, 'Look here, I've had a hard day hunting and I'm just going to have a bath.' This man was an ex-Army officer, a bit blunt in his manner. He fetched the dog and did not thank me, but said, 'When are you going to clean out that ditch next to my field?'

Later in conversation with our police officer, he said, 'Let's summons him.' I said, 'The dogs were not worrying the sheep.' He replied, 'When dogs are loose in a sheep field technically they are worrying.' I smiled and replied, 'My neighbour is chairman of the local petty sessions. Let's forget it!'

It's a poor prospect for a parish when the dogs outnumber the sheep.

I think this true saying comes from A.G. Street. My opinion is that there are far too many dogs about. Having kept them all my life I love dogs.

When dogs are well looked after that is fine. Some of the larger breeds with foreign names are excellent guard dogs, but they do need careful training. Recently at our church the service was conducted by a blind lady. With her she had a golden retriever. While she spoke it lay at her feet for a time. Later, it walked a little away and lay down. That dog knew when the service was over. After the last hymn the lady pronounced the Benediction and the dog immediately got up, went to its mistress and stood while the blind lady put the harness on its back.

A shelter is as good as a meal.

'Gives not the Hawthorn bush a sweeter shade to shepherds looking on their silly sheep than doth a rich embroidered canopy to Kings that fear their subjects' treachery.'

These two sayings come from Shakespeare's *Henry VI, Part 3*. The first regarding shelter is so true. No animal likes wet on its back day after day and in the summer animals thrive where there is shade. I have seen lambs playing on frozen snow but when wet sleet or rain falls on them they need shelter as well as food. The hawthorn bush's shade is not only welcome to Shakespeare's shepherds but to the sheep.

In summer if stock have shade and plenty of water they will thrive regardless of the scarcity of the grass. How I remember being sent up on Bredon Hill as a boy to count the cattle. The summer sun had driven them to shade among the hawthorn bushes. As fast as I counted two or three, they moved and I failed to count them until, walking up on the edge of night they were feeding away from the bushes which had all day protected them from the Bree Fly.

CHAPTER EIGHT

Women, Babies and Chickens

A whistling woman and a crowing hen
Is neither good for God nor men.

A whistling woman was supposed to bring bad luck. The men on the farm were quite horrified if they heard a woman whistling at work, though I have heard women who would whistle a tune beautifully.

Seafaring men in the nineteenth century believed that a woman's whistle would make the wind blow. This was supposed to be good if a ship was becalmed or 'in the Doldrums'. Women sold winds to sailors in the form of cords with three knots in them. When the first knot was loosened a good wind arose, with the second loosened a stronger wind, with the third a gale. In 1814 Sir Walter Scott bought a wind in Stromness from Bessie Mills and recorded it in his diary. However, a whistling woman remained an object of superstitious dread among seafaring men almost down to our own day, because to whistle was a simple magical method of raising the wind. No skipper would allow any female to whistle on his ship. A Scarborough captain in the mid-nineteenth century would not take a young girl on board his vessel because on another occasion he had heard her whistle.

A hen that crowed was the forerunner of disaster on the farm. We kept White Leghorn fowls in the orchard. Some roosted in the fowl house adjoining the cowshed; others roosted in the barn. One winter's morning as I was in the yard with Dad he said to the cowman, 'That cockerel has a peculiar kind of crow.' The cowman replied, 'It's one of Mrs Archer's hens that is crowing and I don't like it. It's an omen.' 'Kill it,' Dad replied and I helped the cowman to corner the hen in the barn and he wrung its neck. 'What will you do with it?' I asked him. 'Bury it in the muck bury. I wouldn't like to eat it,' he replied.

Dressed up like a dog's dinner.

Usually said of women when they dress up to go to church on Sundays. Country folk, if they wear something new, are asked 'Has there been a fire?' inferring that the clothes were bought with insurance money.

I wonder where the saying came from. I cannot think of anything less exciting than a dog's dinner! We fed our dogs on scraps from the dinner table, bones, etc. Sometimes of curse, the saying was meant ironically.

Why shouldn't country folk dress up? The old idea of the straw-sucking, swede-gnawing chap who eats tallow candles is gone for ever, although the fashions in women's clothes are perhaps worn a little later than in the city. I regret that farmers at market today dress not unlike bank managers. That is a pity. I remember Dad going to market in his breeches and leggings and a decent trilby hat. Many of his contemporaries wore bowlers.

One lady in our village was always the height of fashion. A farmer's wife, she bought her clothes in a fashionable store in a nearby town. It is true she often overstepped the mark price-wise in those hard times for farmers in the late twenties, but I would not say that she was dressed up like a dog's dinner. She liked to impress the cottage women and would lose the bill for an outfit in the village street. The women would exclaim, 'Look what Mrs X paid for her outfit!' But they were glad of her cast-offs when the clothes were sold for a few pence at the jumble sale!

Miss Matthews of Ford feeding chickens and ducks

Delaretha Lawrence of Chedworth at the age of fifteen with Mabel Parry, aged ten months, in a pram, 1905

A 'Band of Hope' or other children's group outing in the Bampton area of the Cotswolds, c. 1905–10

Children and chickens must always be picking.

It is odd how over the years children – by children in this instance I mean babies – are fed differently. Not long ago it was the vogue to feed babies at regular intervals. That was good, but today babies are fed when they are hungry. Mothers know the difference between a cry of temper and one of hunger.

'Children and chickens must always be picking' applies to the world in general. A calf fed on its mother sucks many times in twenty-four hours. Young chickens must be fed regularly, not just twice a day like the hens. Older children do not really need to feed so often, but they like to eat between meals and so lose their appetite for the set meal. They must be picking. How often has a child called, 'Mummy, can I have a biscuit? I'm hungry. Can I have a glass of water?' just to claim attention?

As uncertain as a baby's bottom.

This saying can be applied to the weather, to prices, to crops, or to almost anything on the farm.

Babies' bottoms are unpredictable, that is sure! I remember when our eldest daughter was a baby. It was the last winter of the war, a very cold night. We were in Birmingham, and I was carrying the baby to the bus station. All at once I experienced something quite hot against my pullover. She had spent a penny and soon the hot became very cold on that frosty night!

Cows are uncertain. I have noticed that when they are tied to the manger they stand there very quiet for the milking or for the calf to suckle. As soon as you undo their chains and before they leave the cowshed up go their tails and they relieve themselves. It is probably nerves that causes this but if only they would wait until they left the building. . . .

Two women in one house, two cats and one mouse, two dogs and one bone, will never agree for long.

I wonder who thought of this saying – perhaps someone who had experience of these three things!

Two women in one house, both eager to do the housekeeping, can be a problem. The trouble usually arises in the kitchen. Mrs X does the cakes this way, Mrs Y another way. Each woman will assert that she is right and the other wrong. In other parts of the house there can be argument over the dusting: some dust and then hoover, some hoover and then dust. The washing up is done in different ways by folk – one uses the washing-up bowl, the other the sink; one dries straight away, another leaves the crocks to drain. So there is no compromise.

Two cats and one mouse. The cats will spit and swear at each other, their hackles will go up, and just think of the poor mouse! Cats are cruel with mice. They torment and play for a while before the poor mouse is killed. With two cats, one cat is usually the boss and he or she will keep the other from killing the mouse.

Equally two dogs will never agree over one bone for long. After the initial squabble the boss dog will keep the bone, but dogs have a good memory and the fight over the bone will be remembered, the dogs will seldom be friends again.

A woman, a dog, and a Walnut tree, The more you beat them the better they be.

What a load of rubbish! A man who worked for us was knocking walnuts off one of our trees with a stick as he stood on a ladder. He quoted this rhyme to me as he beat the walnut tree. I doubt if he said it to his wife, and a dog that is beaten is a nervous, useless dog.

Doing the last job first.

A neighbouring farmer said to one of his men, 'You are getting married then, Percy.' 'Yes, Gaffer,' he replied, 'I'm marrying the lady who plays the organ at chapel.' The farmer replied, 'Yes, and from what I can see of it you have blowed her organ and that's known as "Doing the last job first"!'

CHAPTER NINE

The Seasons of the Year

The Glastonbury Thorn.

The Thorn of Glastonbury is said to bloom at Christmas. It is supposed to be a tree grown from when Joseph of Arimathea stuck his staff into the ground near Glastonbury Tor. The name has now been given to a variety of hawthorn, which blooms on old Christmas Day, 6 January, a relic of the old calendar which ended in the mid-1700s.

Onion skins very thin mild winter coming in.
Onion skins thick and tough coming winter very rough.

This jingle smacks a bit of the fable that if there is a good crop of hips and haws we shall have a hard winter.

It was excusable for our ancestors to forecast the winter by the thickness of onion skins, but I am afraid the thickness of the skin was due to the weather during the summer growing season.

As the days lengthen so does the cold strengthen.

The days shorten in December and St Thomas's Day (21 December) is the shortest day of the year. It is unusual for winter to take its grip before Christmas. In the new year the days lengthen and it is then the cold strengthens. January is reckoned to be the coldest month.

On St Paul's day half the winter is past and half is to come.

In Yorkshire 14 January, St Hilary's day, is thought to be the coldest day of the year, and by 25 January, St Paul's day, it is believed half the winter is over.

There was a common belief in old times that on the evening of this day a fierce contest took place among the winds and that the wind that proved victorious at midnight would be the prevailing wind all the year.

At New Year's Tide the days lengthen a cock's stride.
At Candlemas an hour wide.
On your farm on Candlemas Day
A farmer should have half his straw and half his hay.

Here is good advice because although at Candlemas, 2 February, the days are getting longer, there is no grazing for animals and winter feeding must continue until May Day. If the weather in December and January has been open with little frost and little snow sometimes the grass does grow a little.

I remember one season when in my fields there was a good lot of foggy old grass and the cattle were quite happy without hay until the new year.

An old farmer friend of mine said, 'With cattle, they seem to lose condition inside before it shows on their coats. Some hay with the grazing keeps them in condition.'

*If Candlemas Day be fair and bright, winter will have
another flight.
But if it be dark with clouds and rain, winter is gone
and won't come again.*

I would not bet on this prediction yet Candlemas is a milestone in
the countryman's year. Men get out in their cottage gardens and
prepare the ground, plant a few peas and broad beans and shallots.

When I was a boy Candlemas was the day of the horse fair,
when Dad bought me my first pony. The first snowdrops are
often to be seen.

A peck of March dust is worth a king's ransom.

A dry March makes the claylands of England bear abundant crops
of corn. If March weather makes the roads dusty it will benefit the
country.

March doesn't finish until the 12th of April.

This old saying, spoken to me by an old countryman, is not so
silly as it sounds, because of the borrowing days when the
calendar was altered – old Christmas Day was 6 January, which
would make our present March finish on 12 April. My old friend
used to say that the cold March winds continued until 12 April.

As mad as a March hare.

Hares do not travel far, they keep to the few fields that they are
accustomed to. In March the Jack hares, or males, perform

A family in the hay field at Yanworth, c. *1910*

A postcard scene of the village school at Salperton, forming part of a row of cottages,
c. *1905*

Workers in the hay field on the Wantage estate at Lockinge, Berkshire, c. 1906

The winter of 1916 at Hampnett on the Fosse Way

peculiar boxing displays as part of their mating act.

The first time I saw them doing this I stood and stared, I could not believe my eyes. They stood on their hind legs and boxed. They jumped over each other and ran around in little circles. The hares were quite oblivious of me and I walked to within a few yards of them. To say they were mad is a bit strong, but folk who act in odd ways are described as 'as mad as a March hare'.

In spring hair is worth more than a meal.

This refers to out-wintered cattle. Cattle that winter out in the fields grow coats like rugs. In the spring they are ready to make use of the grass. Yarded cattle 'go back' – when they are turned out into the fields after a winter in a yard they lose condition for a while. It takes time for them to adjust to the change from dry food to spring grass. Cattle with sleek coats from the yards are not happy when a cold wind in May blows.

Obviously, young cattle are better in a building or yard for the winter, they would not stand the weather. There is one exception, that is in the case of single suckling calves with their mothers. They thrive out of doors if the cow is milking well.

When we sold two-year-old store cattle in the 1920s we always kept the heifers through the winter. The auctioneer would read: 'These cattle have been out-wintered. They are home-bred, warranted barren.' In spring hair is worth more than a meal.

If you don't wear something new on Easter Day the crows will spoil everything you have on.

Here is a saying from Warwickshire. It is threatening, but not to be taken seriously. It has always been the custom to wear new clothes at Easter, to wear a new bonnet at the Easter parade. Little girls going to Sunday School on Easter Sunday wore pretty new frocks, Easter being the time of rebirth when the fields, the hedges and the gardens all spring to life.

May come early, May come late,
It's bound to make the old cow quake.

This must refer to the May blossom or Hawthorn bloom. It is sometimes out at the end of April.

The saying, of course, also means that the weather in May is most fickle. A cold May is bad for animals. I have seen sheep that have been shorn at the end of May standing with their backs up against the cold east wind.

Regarding cattle, May Day – 12 May on the old calendar – is the recognized day to turn the cattle out from the yard to the fields.

Hawthorn bloom and Elder flowers
Will fill the house with evil powers.

It has always been considered very unlucky to take Hawthorn bloom into the house. I like Shakespeare's term 'blow' instead of bloom, a word still used when I was a boy.

Hawthorn, or May, blossom has a particularly heady scent, it follows the blossom of the Blackthorn or Sloe. The term 'Blackthorn Winter' means that as long as the Blackthorn is in flower winter will linger on.

The flower of the Elderberry, or Elder flower, in fact the Elder tree itself, is an object of superstition. The old idea was that if Elder wood was burnt on the fire the Devil would come down the chimney. Men on the farm when I was a boy would never burn Elder wood – called Ellun in Gloucestershire – on their fires. There is a legend that Judas hanged himself on an Elder tree and that put a spell on the tree, the wood and the blossom. A pity, Elder flowers make a good wine known as Elder Champagne, and the berries make both wine and jam. The flowers when laced into the bridles of working horses keep the flies away on hot sunny days.

Cast not a clout till May is out.

This is an old warning not to shed winter clothing too early. Here again, it refers to the May blossom on the hedges.

Oats in May make a man run away,
Oats in June sing a different tune.

Here is observation. The rain of winter followed by the cold winds make oats turn a bad colour, yellow in the leaf. This is known as 'May sickness'. The warmer weather in June brings back their colour. Today the application of nitrate fertilizer does this.

Cut a thistle in June it will bloom again soon.
Cut a thistle in July it will lie down and die.

This is true but by leaving this until July they will be seeding and spreading themselves over the land.

He sucks little birds' eggs to make his voice clear,
And when he sings 'cuckoo' the summer is near.

Here is a saying from the Forest of Dean.
  Of course, the countryman can tell a cuckoo a mile away. For

several years running I used to read in a local paper that someone in Cheltenham had heard a cuckoo in March. It was probably a Collared Dove. The cuckoo does not come to Gloucestershire much before 19 April.

The arrival of this bird does mean that summer is near. Our ancestors would have liked summer all the year round and so would we! They made cuckoo pens to fence the birds in so that they could not return to the south. They feed on insects so I doubt if they lived long when autumn came followed by winter.

When you hear the cuckoo shout
It's time to plant your taters out.

That is not bad advice. The third week in April is a good time to plant lots of things. Good Friday has been the time to plant early potatoes but Easter is a movable feast. When Easter is late the cuckoo could be here.

In the south of England years ago no one worked on Good Friday, but potato planting was the usual job in the midlands that day. On an estate near where I was born the squire told his men that they could have Good Friday as a holiday providing that they went to church first. When the men neglected to go to church the squire cancelled the holiday!

Cold weather is a good gaffer

Men work hard to keep warm and do more work without prompting from the gaffer.

CHAPTER TEN

Neighbours

Love thy neighbour but pull not down thy hedge.

Here is good advice! There has always been trouble between
neighbours regarding boundaries to properties and fences and
while neighbours should be friendly, to get what is known as 'too
thick' with neighbours is a mistake. Farmers do borrow tools and
implements from their neighbours, that is all right but no one likes
to be taken for granted. I knew a farmer who would borrow an
implement from a neighbour without asking permission. He kept
it and often his neighbour had to fetch it back when he wanted to
use it himself. There was a case when the farmer had a farm sale of
his implements and livestock – one or two of them belonged to
my father who sent me to fetch them from the sale field. The
implements had already got the sale numbers stuck on them.

Give and take among neighbours is a good thing. We borrowed
wagons from neighbours at haymaking; they would borrow our
mowing machine. When I visited one good neighbour every
spring he would say, 'I know what you have come to borrow, the
seed barrow. It's in the barn.' That seed barrow, or drill, used to
go around most of the village.

Good fences make good neighbours.

This makes strong sense. It is probably not common knowledge
that when the Inclosure Acts were made law this made the
boundary between enclosed fields a ditch. A ditch was dug to
mark the boundary and to drain the land, then the soil from the

ditch was thrown up on to the side of the field and a hedge planted on the bank of soil. Both the hedge and the ditch, which was on his neighbour's side of the hedge were the responsibility of the farmer who owned the enclosed land. There have been and always will be disputes about exactly where the dividing boundary is.

Some countrymen reckon that apart from the hedge and the ditch the farmer owns a few feet on the neighbour's side of the ditch. Farmers and their men when out shooting draw the hedge and ditch for game and rabbits and believe, rightly or wrongly, that one of the guns is within his rights to walk on his neighbour's land and that if a shot bird falls on his neighbour's land he is entitled to retrieve it but must not take his gun with him in doing so. It is all very complicated.

In many places, particularly towns, there are joint-owned hedges between properties, yet some garden fences are owned and maintained on one side of the garden and the other side is the responsibility of the neighbour.

In the midlands the clayland fields are what is known as 'landed up'. The high ridges of the plough lands and the deep furrows make a pattern like barrows. If the 'Lands', as they are called, run from east to west, the southern side gets more sun and is considerably warmer than the northern slope. In pasture fields the ants always build their mounds, what we called 'ant humps', on the southern slope.

Field drains in the furrows between the lands either empty into the ditch at the edge of the field or into a master drain. Some of these field drains are quite old. The older ones were half-piped but later on cylindrical two- or three-inch pipes were used.

A field near a council housing estate was laid out for allotments. The tenants were allocated a 'Land' each. The 'Lands' were about six yards wide and fifty yards long. There were no boundary fences, each allotment holder knew where his boundary was. In any case, had there been a hedge that would have taken up valuable land for growing vegetables.

Alf and Bert were neighbours. Whether by accident or design Bert kept encroaching on to Alf's land, a bit more every year,

The butcher's van brings neighbours out in the street in Bledington in the Cotswolds

A man feeding three black pigs

A group of villagers and the postman outside the postbox in Little Wolford, near Shipston-on-Stour, c. 1910

when he planted his crops. Alf said, 'Look here, Bert, you have trespassed on to my land with your sprouts. You have come over about four feet.' 'Never,' Bert replied. 'We will prove where the boundary is,' and with these words Alf took a spade to dig down to find the drainpipe which lay in the furrow between the Lands. The three-inch pipe was found about four feet from where Bert had encroached onto Alf's Land. There was no argument, that was the boundary.

Another important point here is that 'Every farmer must fence against his own stock'. This makes it difficult if his neighbour's fence is not stock-proof. Here we have a problem: Farmer X keeps sheep and the fence between his land and Farmer Y belongs to the latter, who is an arable farmer. His fence is reasonably well clipped, but not sheep-proof. Farmer X's sheep get through the fence belonging to Farmer Y who naturally complains of damage to his crop. 'The fence belongs to you, Farmer Y,' says Farmer X. That is as may be but he must fence against his own stock. To be sure his stock will not stray may mean having to erect a fence on his land if his neighbour does not repair the boundary fence. I have been blessed with some good neighbours.

Remove not the ancient landmark which your fathers have set up.

These old words from the Bible are applicable today. Churches, trees, old buildings, crosses, all play their part in the beauty of today's countryside. New landmarks are the triangulation stones which are set up on high points to denote elevations.

CHAPTER ELEVEN

Pigs and Geese

As fierce as Cox's pig.

This saying comes from Cutsdean on the Cotswolds. My friend
Geoff used it in the 1930s. It is meant to describe someone
who is as it describes – fierce. Why Cox's pig was fierce is a
mystery.

Most cottagers kept a pig for bacon. It is true boar pigs
can become fierce. Joe Whittle, an expert pig killer, told me
that he was called to kill a boar pig. He went towards the sty
where the pig was and he said it roared like a lion and had long
tusks. The owner said he had not dared to go in to the pig for
some months but fed it over the gate. Joe had to shoot it with a
rifle.

The quietest sow sups the most wash.

Someone who was observant coined this saying. It is noticeable
that the quiet animal eats her meal, or wash, and thrives on it
whereas an animal that is forever making a noise and running
about here and there loses out.

The saying, of course, is also meant to refer to people. We have
all seen the businessman who is very quiet but has a listening ear.
A man who never brags, keeps his own counsel, succeeds; a
fellow, or woman, who is forever telling the world what they are
doing often fails.

Yes, the quietest sow sups the most wash.

It takes a good breed of pig to eat acorns.

This is a saying from the Forest of Dean where the men kept pigs in the woods besides the sheep. Free range pigs eat so many things. They will enjoy roots of blackberry bushes, root up bluebells and eat acorns.

A good pig for the Forest is the Gloucester Old Spot, a native of these woods, sometimes known as the Orchard Pig. They will eat quantities of apples.

Foresters are hardy, they live and thrive, where softer mortals would die.

Kill a pig when the moon is waxing. If you kill when the moon is on the wane half the bacon will fry away in the pan.

This old saying was really adhered to in the last century. The country calendar was based on custom and saints' days, and country folk studied the moon before killing their pigs in March each year. Farley Archer, Grandfather's cousin, was keen on working with the moon. He also planted his seeds when the moon was waxing.

There are more ways to kill a pig than hang him.

It is a bit obscure this one, I have heard it said so many times on the farm. For instance, if Tom the cowman had a cow which kicked and he needed some milk for the house, he would put the cow's calf to suckle on one side and milk her on the other. The cow would not kick at her own calf. Hence the saying which he used in this situation: There are more ways to kill a pig than hang him.

Pigs can see wind.

This fallacy comes from the fact that pigs behave strangely in a gale. They do not like wind.

There are as many ways to cut up a bacon pig as there are pigs.

A bacon pig killer told me this when he had killed a pig for me during the war. 'How do you want it cut up?' he asked me. He called the backbone the 'Christening Chines'. I replied: 'Use your own discretion.' 'Discretion be damned!' he replied, 'There are as many ways to cut up a pig as there are pigs.'

What is sauce for the goose is also sauce for the gander.

This well-known saying refers to equal treatment for all, especially between husband and wife. Our roadman, Stodge Warren, was by the village green, when the churchwarden came along and asked him, 'Who has been driving their car over the Green?' The car's wheels had made deep ruts on the grass. Stodge replied, 'Oh, it was the Reverend.'

The vicar was the churchwarden's brother-in-law and he said: 'What is sauce for the goose is also sauce for the gander, I will have a word with the vicar.'

CHAPTER TWELVE

The Working Man

Every generation gets weaker and wiser.

There is some truth in this saying. Up until 1946 when grain was harvested by the reaper/binder, wheat was put into sacks of 2 cwt 28 lb, beans in sacks of 2 cwt 42 lb. These sacks had to be man-handled. Men earlier in the century were used to carrying weights such as this, they had no option, but they often suffered later from it with hernias and they had little help in those days before the National Health Service.

One can argue that the present generation is weaker and wiser. I would not say that they are weaker. Folk today can run faster, jump higher, jump longer than their fathers and grandfathers. They are wiser. The law forbids a workman to lift heavy weights and the fact is that there are machines to do much of the heavy work.

I remember sulphate of ammonia fertilizer coming in 2 cwt sacks. Builders' labourers had to contend with 2 cwt sacks of cement. It was foolish. Thank God men are wiser today.

Wear the old 'uns out first.

This was first said to me when as a boy I first started work on the land. At the end of a long day horse hoeing with George we had finished hoeing the field just by the gate. Our food baskets, called 'fittle baskets' by George, were at the other end of the field, where we had eaten our bait and dinner. George said, 'Now then, you be younger than me, go and fetch the fittle baskets.' I only had to look at him a bit downcast and he started to walk to the other side of the field to fetch our baskets. Then he commented, 'Wear the old 'uns out first.'

There are more people rust out than wear out.

This could be true today, but in the days of manual work on the land the men did not rust – their hard lives wore them out.

Hard work never killed anyone.

This is not really true. I have seen men who worked themselves to death.

He talks as his belly guides him.

He's got more to say than he's got to eat.

These sayings seem to contradict each other.

The first saying is obvious, it speaks of a man who has been drinking. Men under the influence of drink do vary. Some go very sleepy and say little, they just long to sleep it off; others are stupid yet jolly and will sing and talk and presumably are happy. These last can also be quarrelsome and threatening. Some say they cannot take drink without being argumentative or aggressive, and there is a school of thought which says that men who are quarrelsome when under the influence of drink are quite often no better when sober!

The second saying describes a boastful person – with not much to boast about!

Teddy Vale outside his cottage at Grafton in the late 1920s. He was an expert sower and reaper, and with the Evesham Two Tine Digger he was able to dig 484 square yards in a day

The miller's wagon at Bourton-on-the-Water mill

Jack Hunting, a rough carpenter, making pit props on Bredon Hill during the First World War

Cousin George, winner of the 1937 sprout-picking championships at Charlton, near Pershore, photographed at Overbury. On the left stands the author's father, Tom Archer; on the right, Mr Cartwright, of Harvey's of Kidderminster, who supplied the fertilizer

One boy will work for you, two boys are half a boy, three boys are no boy at all.

A conundrum you may rightly say, but it is so true. A boy working with the farm men is good to have on the land. He is inexperienced yet a good boy is willing to learn and he is expected to do the boring jobs on the farm. When two boys work together it is natural than they will get up to mischief and can be more a hindrance than a help, so two boys equal half a boy. Regarding three boys, I have experience of three boys together on a farm!

It was a wet day in July. Frank and Geoff were with me cutting stinging nettles in a field known as Ten Furlongs. We were all about sixteen years old. Frank cut his hand on a bagging hook, a kind of sickle. He was sharpening his hook with a whetstone when it slipped. Geoff and I were wrapping up his finger and talking together in a group in the middle of the field. Dad's partner was in his bedroom changing into his market clothes to go to town. He saw from his window that we were not getting on with cutting the nettles and thistles in Ten Furlong. 'What's going on?' the farmer called from the window. 'Frank has cut his finger,' I replied. 'But you three have not cut many thistles or nettles all the morning. You will have to be parted. Frank, you go up on the Leasow cutting thistles up there. Geoff, you go along to the Ham and cut thistles there and Fred, you stay in Ten Furlong.' Of course we missed the company of each other but we probably did more work. It is nearly sixty years ago now.

Swopping knives.

This is hindering time. We were carting mangolds from the field to the bury. I took the horse and cart load of mangolds part-way and met Frank with an empty cart which I took back to the field. We stopped and had a chin wag. Dad caught us and he said, 'Don't you boys hinder too much time swopping knives.'

A shilling, a knife and a piece of string. You can cut, tie and buy.

These were considered the three essentials. As a boy on the farm I was told to carry these three things by Tom our cowman. Boys carry all sorts of things in their pockets and for me a knife and a piece of string were a must. I had not always got a shilling!

A knife came in handy to paunch and hock a rabbit, to cut a stick, made a catapult, and cut the string. String, that is binder twine, would make a belt around my coat, a temporary shoe lace or even braces, tie up a gate, or tie a withy pole to repair (temporarily) a fence. A lot could be bought for a shilling in the 1920s. It was probably worth a pound in today's money.

It wouldn't cut butter if it was made red hot. I could ride bare-assed to London on it without being cut.

Sayings from our carter about a blunt skim share or any other cutting tool. Exaggerations if you like, yet they have been said but never tried!

Some turn up their sleeves to work, others turn up their noses.

When I started work on the land I soon learnt to turn up my shirt sleeves. One man who worked in our gang never turned up his sleeves. He was constantly being reminded about it. There seemed to be a code regarding clothes on the land. Men wore flannel undershirts even in summer. They never took off their shirts in hot weather.

I was told about a chap who applied to Dad for a job on the farm. He was wearing a collar and tie. Dad and his partner did not give him a job. They said that a man in a collar and tie did not look like a good worker.

When pleasure do become a business it do usually turn sour.

A wise old saying from the Forest of Dean, and so true. We have all seen the results in sport. A little football team turns professional and loses its community spirit. A small agricultural show which was held on a bank holiday expands and goes on for two days with roped off sections for 'members only'. The show ceases to be local, competitors come from far and wide. Pleasure becomes a business and turns sour.

CHAPTER THIRTEEN

Children's Sayings at Play

Two, four, six, eight, ten,
Shoot a badger, Amen.

A game played by boys when I was at school was called 'Tag a Bummer'. One boy stood against a wall propping up three more bending as for leap frog. Another three boys tried to jump on top of the other team. If they succeeded they called 'Two, four, six, eight, ten, shoot a badger, Amen.'

Salt, Mustard, Vinegar, Pepper.

This was a girls' skipping rhyme common in Lancashire. They started skipping slowly but got faster when they called 'pepper'.

Finger wet, finger dry,
Cut my throat before I die.

This was said by children in Worcestershire to prove they spoke the truth: the child wet his forefinger and put it across his throat.

> *Donald Duck was hung up,*
> *Broke a saucer and a cup.*

Another skipping rhyme.

> *Each peach pear plum out goes number one.*
> *Each peach pear plum out goes number two. And so on.*

> *Dip, dip, dip. Your blue ship sailing on the water.*
> *Like a cup and saucer you're not it.*

These are two of the numerous counting-out sayings, the rhymes used to select the child to have first go at games such as batting at cricket, or to pick teams for rounders.

> *Eany, Meany, Miney, Mo.*
> *Catch a black boy by the toe.*
> *If he squeals let him go.*
> *Eany, Meany, Miney, Mo.*

We used this rhyme when we played hide-and-seek. The last one left went to the den, which might be a tree, and closed his or her eyes and counted to a hundred while the other children went away to hide. If they were found and could not get back to the tree they were out. If they got back to the tree before the others they called: 'My den, one, two, three. Barley or Pax'. All very involved! Then we sang:

> When I was a boy and had no sense,
> I bought a fiddle for eighteen pence
> And the only tunes that I could play
> Was Sally get out of the donkey's way.

I'm the King of the castle.
Get down you dirty rascal.

This was called out by a boy or girl when they stood high up on a fence or on a hay rick. The other children tried to dislodge him or her and claim 'King of the castle' for themselves.

Obbildy, obbildy, onkher,
My first conker.
Obbildy, obbildy, oh,
My first go.

This was recited before a game of conkers or 'obbildy onkhers'. The players had three strokes each with their horse-chestnuts to try and break their opponent's nut or knock it off its string. When the game finished the players totted up their scores. If the victor's opponent's nut had already conquered five others the five would be added to the victor's tally. Some nuts won as many as twenty conquests. Boys used to bake their horse-chestnuts in the oven to make them hard. If the competitors' strings got entangled, the first one to shout 'strings' had the next strike.

Sally go round the sun.
Sally go round the moon.
Sally go round the chimney pot on a Sunday afternoon.

A children's saying used when we played rounders.

CHAPTER FOURTEEN

Haymaking and Harvest

Ham and eggs mind your legs,
Bread and cheese take your ease.

Here's a saying which must go back well over a hundred years, to when Grandfather mowed the riverside meadows with a scythe. In those days gangs of men went mowing, working piecework or by the acre. A good man could mow an acre a day. The mowers stayed overnight in the barns and the farmer provided them with food. Some farmers were generous and fed the men well. Then the men worked hard, and as they worked they recited: 'Ham and eggs mind your legs.' When the farmer was mean they recited: 'Bread and cheese take your ease.'

There was an art to mowing. The important thing was to keep the knoll, or heel, of the scythe down low on the ground. Good mowers worked that way and saved time by not sticking the point of the scythe blade in the ground. Another trick was to put a long edge on the scythe with the whetstone so that the edge lasted longer, avoiding the necessity of having to stop to sharpen the scythe.

With horses, it was common practice to put the colt in the middle of the team. When Grandfather's team were mowing with their scythes they put the learner, or colt, in front. He had to work hard because the older mower behind him would mow close to his heels and egg him along.

T'whet to cut, t'whet to cut,
The mowers are so lazy.
A pint of beer will make um drunk
A quart will make um crazy.

This was a humorous jingle recited by farmers when whetting their scythe blades, and strikes me as a reference to the bread and cheese type of farmer. Mowers in the hayfield usually drank cider and not beer. Men were allowed a gallon of cider each a day at haymaking and harvest, twice the amount allowed at other times. One farmer I knew gave his men what was known as 'small beer', a weak drink which would never make the men drunk or crazy.

The cattle in the winter would rather eat this hay than
their fore feet or a snow ball.

This was said in a wet awkward haymaking season when the rain off and on spoilt the hay. Every time hay is turned in the swath and it rains the hay becomes less palatable and is discoloured and if it is damp in the rick it will either go mouldy or get hot. It is much better if it heats up a little, then it gets what is known as a 'nose' and smells a bit like tobacco.

When the hay was second-rate men used to say 'It will be good enough for the store cattle'. I thought store cattle would like good fodder as well as the milking cows or the calves, but the store cattle did have to feed on the poor hay.

Over the last few years more and more barley straw has been fed to cattle. It is much better fodder than poor hay.

More hay is spoiled in a good season than in a bad one.

This refers to the fact that when the sun shines farmers are impatient and rick the hay too soon. If it contains a lot of clover it

Hay raking

Harvesting with a crook stick and reap hook in Herefordshire about 1890

Ricks on staddle stones at Grafton. The small rick on the left is straw to keep the staddles dry ready for another rick

Steam threshing at University Farm, Hailey near Witney in Oxfordshire, c. 1910

will 'go back' and get too hot in the rick. I have noticed that on a sunny June day new-mown hay appears dry and made, yet when the sun goes down in the evening it goes back and becomes what is known as 'gay'.

A farmer who who never made a hot rick never made any good hay.

This sounds contradictory but to know when to carry hay is a matter of experience. By letting the hay stay an extra day in the sun, which bleaches it, the fodder loses its goodness and becomes no better than straw. One has to strike the happy medium.

Good hay hath no fellow.

I do not think anything in the country smells as sweet as new-mown hay, especially if it contains all sorts of herbs from an old pasture. If hay can be cut and carried in in about three days without any rain, the cattle in the winter will not leave any in their mangers.

Today silage has largely replaced hay. The feed value of good silage when analyzed is better than the best hay, but badly-made silage positively stinks.

Cuckoo oats and Woodcock hay
Make a farmer run away.

The cuckoo comes about 19 April; when lambs are born after that they are known as 'cuckoo lambs'. To sow oats after 19 April is pushing it a bit. It is late and if the spring is dry and cold the oats will never do much good.

I remember some late oats sown on Bredon Hill in 1931. The sheaves were very short and light, partly due to the rabbits at that time. They were too short to stook so they lay where the binder left them. I had a day with the cowman turning them so that they would dry on the other side. Later, we brought them down the hill on the wagons. When Ralph our carter and I were bringing the last load down the rough track above Grafton the load slipped and tipped over in a gateway. Ralph walked back to the farm to get some help to reload the oats, while I stayed to look after the horses. It was a disastrous crop.

Cuckoo oats are too late in most seasons and yet it is surprising how crops will mature in favourable weather.

Woodcock hay is hay carried in October when the Woodcock is in season. Hay made as late is better than nothing for winter feed, but it lacks the goodness of June hay. We built a rick in September one year but the problem with drying it is the morning dew.

The beans are in flower.

A catchphrase intended to account for a person's silliness. Our forefathers imagined that the perfume of bean flowers made people silly or light-headed. It is similar to August being called 'the silly season'. The perfume of bean flowers is rather special, a heady scent. A field of beans in flower in summer gives a good country smell. Last summer I passed a field in the car, and opened the window to enjoy the scent. Then a field of oil seed rape glowed in blossom, bright yellow in the sun. The scent was overpowering, quite unpleasant and started my nose and throat burning like hay fever.

John Drinkwater in one of his poems, 'The Feckenham Men', seems to know of the peculiar features attributed to bean blossom.

Here is a part of his poem:

> The jolly men of Feckenham one day
> When Summer strode in power,
> Went down it seems among their lands
> And saw their bean field all in flower.
> Wheat ricks they said be good to see
> What would a rick of blossoms be?
> So straight they brought their sickles out
> And worked all day till day was done
> And builded them a good square rick
> Of scented bloom beneath the sun.
> And was not this I tell to you
> A fury hearted thing to do?

I'll give him beans.

If he gives me peas I will give him beans.

To give beans speaks of the threshing of one man to another. Beans were threshed by the flail years after the invention of the threshing machine. 'Beans' suggests something drastic or violent. The second saying indicates tit for tat, or like for like.

The frost has given my peas beans.

The frost has killed the pea blossom, thus ruining the crop.

CHAPTER FIFTEEN

The Farmer and the Land

Three things you will never see in life:

1. A dead donkey.
2. A gipsy wearing glasses.
3. A poor farmer.

This is not to be taken seriously!

I have never seen a dead donkey yet my Grandfather's cousin, Farley Archer, had a donkey which died. He was reputed to have buried his donkey with its four legs sticking up in the air and to have grown runner beans up the donkey's legs.

A gipsy with glasses I cannot recall. These days some gipsies may wear spectacles. In the past gipsies led an open-air life, did little reading and, who knows, may have used some salve from the hedgerows to help them retain good vision.

As for a poor farmer, I have seen many. When prices are good everyone says what a lot of money farmers are making; when prices are bad in years of depression it is a different story, they cannot quit but they must carry on. I remember one year my brother had a good crop of leeks and the price was high. Someone said to me, 'Your brother is making a lot of money with his leeks.' I replied, 'Yes, but don't forget he had to plough them back in the ground the last two years. There was no demand for leeks then.'

A team of three horses haymaking on the Batsford estate, near Moreton-in-Marsh

A sheep fair at Chipping Campden in the early years of the century

Hop-picking in Sussex in 1900

Cider-makers with a ten hogshead barrel

*'One talks of mildew and of frost
And one of storms and hail
And one of pigs that he has lost
By maggots in the tail.'*

William Cowper wrote these lines many years ago, but things do not change much. Some folk still think of farmers living in summer with new-mown hay and strawberries and cream, and in winter sitting by log fires after days hunting and shooting. No, life on the land is not like that for the farmer or his men. They must feed the cattle, break the ice on the water troughs, and cut kale on frosty mornings.

For the townsman, I am sure the subjects talked about by farmers at market or in the pub must be boring. Today the farmer also talks about the protein in his silage, the litres of milk his cows produce. He is more sophisticated but basically he talks of his work.

The poet Gordon Bottomley penned these apt words:

His acre brought forth roots last year.
This year it bears the gleaming grain.
Next spring shall seedling grass appear.
Then roots and corn and grass again.

*'Who skims his milk until it's blue,
And then adds chalk and water too,
And when he pulls his apple crop
Puts the largest on the top?
The honest farmer.'*

These are words of Tusser who wrote them in his book *Five Hundred Points of Good Husbandry* in the sixteenth century. We like to think that times have changed, but in the time when I was a boy

75

amongst old men on the farm Tusser's words rang sadly true.

A farmer who lived in a nearby town and retailed milk had a bad name for the butter fat in his bucket. When Friesian cows first became popular their milk was something over 3 per cent fat. This farmer kept Shorthorns and the analysis should have been much higher. The dairyman, Charlie, used to shout up and down Bridge Street at Evesham, 'Milk Ho, Milk Ho'. Some of the hobble-dehoys (teenagers) at that time knew that Charlie watered his milk, and they echoed his cries and when he called 'Milk Ho' they called 'and', just 'and'. When he chased them they called 'water'. The dairyman got away with it for some time until an inspector of weights and measures approached Charlie for a sample from his bucket. The wily dairyman, knowing that the milk had been watered, tripped over on the pavement, and the milk ran into the gutter. Charlie shouted to the inspector, 'I'm sorry, sir, I haven't got a spot left.'

The saw that Tusser made about the apple crop reminds me of the Vale of Evesham in the 1920s when topping was accepted as common practice. Shopkeepers wanted the best strawberries placed on top of the 1 lb punnets, and we picked strawberries in this manner. Three punnets were placed in a chip basket side by side: in one punnet we put the very best berries, the toppers; the second held the ordinary fruit; the third held the small or jam strawberries. When the punnet containing the ordinary or medium fruit held roughly three-quarters of a pound, the toppers were put on top to finish the 1 lb of strawberries. The small jam strawberries were packed separately. In Cheltenham market the sight of the topped strawberries in trays of twenty-four punnets, with strawberry leaves placed between the punnets to show them off, was a picture. I remember one fruiterer who kept a high-class shop in the Promenade bought a lot of our fruit at those early morning markets in Cheltenham. Obviously this practice was not honest yet the fruit that was put up for sale was all good quality. People in those days knew that the fruit was topped. It used to be said in the Vale of Evesham that there is a trick in every trade except market gardening, in which you will never find the fruit in the middle of the basket better than the fruit on the top.

Some ways of practising topping were really bad. For instance, when plums were packed in 12 lb baskets the ripe ones were put on top. This rarely deceived the merchants in the market, however – they would tip the fruit from one basket to another when it was about to be sold to reveal the true quality.

One very bad case of unfair packing came to light in Evesham market about twenty-five years ago. Small growers pride themselves on the attractive way in which they pack their sprouts for market. The sprouts on the outside of the net are made to look so good. That is fair enough as long as the sprouts inside the net are also of good quality. On this occasion there were twenty nets for sale from a small grower. The merchant tipped the sprouts on to a table in the market and found greens known in the trade as 'blowers' and pieces of stem in the pack. The merchant, who had already bought the sprouts at 15s per net when he tipped them on to the table, called the auctioneer. The auctioneer agreed that the grower had been guilty of deceitful packing and put the sprouts up for sale again. No one bid but he knew a merchant who would repack the vegetables and he called out 'Charlie, 4 shillings', adding, 'I'll teach the grower a lesson.'

Another unfair practice I have seen is the system of over-stocking of cows. When cows were offered for sale in the market they used not to be milked the evening before the scale. Their udders often dripped milk to give an exaggerated appearance of their milk yield. As a young farmer I got caught out in this way buying a heifer in the market which was supposed to have calved a dead calf. The super udder was distended and it looked capable of rearing two calves with ample milk. The heifer had been what is known as 'stanked', i.e. not milked – I milked her when we got her home but next morning she had almost no milk and had to go as barren.

Butchers today are not silly when a fat beast in the market is weighed over the weighbridge and weighs more that anticipated. If the beast has had a big meal of mangolds, the butcher makes allowances.

It is good practice in farming to give good weight but some men soak their vegetables in water. When they drain and dry them they will be short weight. This reminds me of Cousin George who used to say when a sack was overweight that it had 'Malvern measure'.

———

A farmer should live as though he was going to die tomorrow and farm as if he was going to live for ever.

Here is a bit of a puzzle. Yet fundamentally it is good advice, a moral code which takes care of life on and off the farm.

Let us concentrate on the farming aspect of this proverb, 'To farm as if he was going to live for ever'. Farming is a long-term project. A farmer who purges his land with chemicals and pays no attention to the lifelong prospect is short-sighted. A good farmer lays his hedges every seven years, lops his willow trees, regularly cleans his ditches, attends to his drains. These somewhat mundane jobs are not directly connected with the production of the farm, but if neglected the farm will suffer.

In the cleaning of arable land I was always told of the importance of keeping the headlands clean. It is from the headlands that the weeds creep over the field. It is so patently true that the land is only on loan. Someone comes after the farmer and reaps the benefit of his good farming or suffers from his bad husbandry.

It is a debatable point as to how long it takes to build up a good dairy herd or a flock of sheep. I do remember that after Dad had an outbreak of foot-and-mouth disease among his cows, he never built up a similar herd.

With the advent of heavy tractors the work of ploughing is not shown in real horse-power terms. I know a farm where the farmer used farmyard manure and rotated his crops, and two horses could plough the land easily. After years of application of nitrates with little organic manure it took four horses in line to plough the now heavy land. This loss of the humus and a change in the texture of the land is not so apparent in the tractor age.

My uncle farmed as if he was going to live for ever. In his mid-seventies he pulled up his apple trees and planted plum trees. I wondered at the time whether he would reap the benefit. He lived to be ninety-five and saw his plum trees in full bearing.

One years seeding, seven years weeding.

It is so important to keep the land clean to grow food crops. Weeds do persist and it is important never to let them seed. This used to be done with the hoe, now chemicals are used.

CHAPTER SIXTEEN

Horses and Ploughing

Never look a gift-horse in the mouth.

Up until a horse is about six years old its age can be told by its teeth. After the age of six it is difficult to assess. To look a gift-horse in the mouth is an insult to the giver.

Some years ago my daughter had an Exmoor pony. I knew when I bought the animal at market that it was aged. It was probably twenty years old, but it served for my daughter to ride. It was what is known as 'long in the tooth'. A chap was working for me who had served in the Royal Army Veterinary Corps in the First World War. He asked me one day, 'Would you like me to make the pony into a four-year-old?' 'What!' I replied. 'It's long in the tooth, grey around its muzzle. It's an old pony.' Being inquisitive to hear what Charlie proposed in his comical way, I did however ask him what he could do. He replied, 'If I took so many teeth out of the pony and filed the others down it would appear to be four years old.'

Perhaps some horse copers, or dealers, have done this doubtful thing. Of course it is deceitful.

Sometimes young horses die. Old horses are bound to.

Here is a very true saying. It applies not only to horses but to all animals, including humans.

During the war I had a mare named Bounce. She was about six years old, a lovely Shire and a good worker. Just before harvest Bounce got out of her pasture into a field of wheat. She ate a

A four-horse ploughing team

Horse and cart in a farmyard at Coln St Dennis

A young carter with a Shire horse

Ploughing with oxen in the Cotswolds

quantity of young wheat and died. Horses' stomachs, in contrast to those of cows, have a small intestine and if this becomes clogged with the paste of wheat, it soon proves fatal. My old nag Tom lived to be thirty-five years old. Bounce was just six years old. 'Sometimes young horses die. Old horses are bound to.' Death is one thing that is sure to happen eventually.

What kills old horses is starting work again.

When an old horse is turned out and more or less pensioned off it is fatal then to put it to a hard day's work. To use an old horse in a cart to fetch a load of mangolds from the bury is not a bad thing, it keeps him active. Horses, both old and young, must be treated sensibly, though.

Young horses were put to work on the land for a short period at two to three years old. After the initial breaking-in they were then turned up. A carter I knew told me that the first work they did at the plough made them sweat because they were what he called green. When they were turned up in the field afterwards the horses grew stronger until they were five years old.

The saying can also be applied to people. I have known men who left the hard grind of farm work take a job in a factory. When I asked one man I knew how he liked the change in his job, he replied, 'If I had to work twice as hard it would not be as bad as land work.' I looked at him and thought, 'He doesn't look too well.' Soon afterwards he died. He may well have died had he worked on the farm once more, 'Starting again'.

A mare and a hare go just twelve months.

I wondered about this saying when first I heard it. A hare surely does not go twelve months before the leverets are born. The truth is, of course, a mare goes eleven months from the time she has been served by a stallion, and a hare one month from the time the jack hare serves her.

A good horse is never a bad colour.

This old saying is true. I can think of so many horses of all colours that have proved to be good horses.

With Shire horses the favourite colour is black, the Black Horse of the midlands. The best horse I had for working was Prince and he was a light brown colour. Flower, a dark chestnut mare, had a colt called Boxer. He was chestnut and not the best of workers. No, colour does not come into it at all. We had a little horse, black with a white face, called Blackbird. He was blind in one eye but he was a willing worker. I also remember two strawberry roan cart horses belonging to a neighbour – fine animals that worked well.

Plough Monday next after that twelfth tide is past
Bids out with the plough the worst husband is last.
If ploughman get hatchet or whip to the shrene
Maids loseth their cocks if water be seen.

In the old days no ploughing was done in the new year until Plough Monday, 6 January. It was on that day that a race took place between the ploughman and the maid. The maid was promised a cockerel to be given to her on Shrove Tuesday for a feast before Lent. To earn this reward she had to have a kettle of water boiled before the ploughman could get to the kitchen with his hatchet or whip.

Plough early till 10 o'clock then to the hay.
In ploughing and carting prompt ye may.
By little and little thus doing ye win.
That plough shall not hinder when harvest comes in.

Farmers cannot arrange work on the farm like a factory. Weather conditions govern every operation. Here we have a common-sense attitude to the job in hand. By ploughing until ten o'clock and then going to the hay field, the hay will have had time for the dew to dry. No farmer would start working with the hay at the crack of dawn when there was still a heavy dew.

By working as the poet describes the horses would be busy all day. After the plough team is unhitched at ten o'clock the horses would be put between the wagon shafts or used as trace horses to help to pull the loads of hay. The carter and his boy would pitch and load the hay.

I remember a day in June when I led the horse, horse-hoeing the beans, until bait time at ten o'clock. After bait my job was horse-raking the hay in the brookside meadow.

CHAPTER SEVENTEEN

Sayings about Folk

As artful as a wagon load of monkeys.

Some folk are artful, some just lucky, their bread always falls with the butter side up.

One man I knew had an employer who was a lay reader at the church. This man would read his Bible in front of his employer at lunchtime just to curry favour.

Not worth a hatful of crabs.

This saying, often spoken to me about folk, crops, or animals, puzzled me. We lived eighty miles from the sea and never saw a crab. Then Tom, our cowman, told me that crabs were lice, so I realized it meant that some thing or body was worse than worthless.

He carves his meat so thin it tastes of the knife.

Occasionally one does meet folk so mean. A man I knew used to charge his wife for the eggs the hens laid. Another man who delivered poultry meal from his mill would take several minutes to undo the tie around the sack so that he could keep the pieces of string. To offer to cut the string would offend him.

As tight as a duck's ass, and that's water tight.

yet

Economy begins at the mouth of the sack.

It is the same thing over again, meanness which is degrading in folk. It has often been said about such people that they had had a good hiding when they were young for giving something away.

As handy as a toad with side pockets.

Like a toad on a hurdle.

As awkward as a tup.

As silly as a sheep.

These derogatory sayings were commonplace on the farm between the wars. Not complimentary, yet they were often said to boys from school who had just started to work on the land. What a toad with side pockets is I hate to think!

We have lived too long in the woods to be frightened by owls.

The folk of the Forest of Dean, where this saying comes from, are known to be a hardy race, and living as they do between two rivers, the Severn and the Wye, makes them folk apart.

What, frightened by owls? The bird life in the Forest is still spectacular. To walk through these woods is to be in the company of birds of all kinds: the sound of the woodpecker, the laughing call of the jay, the wood pigeon, or quist as it is known in Gloucestershire, with his pathetic call 'My toe bleeds Betty'.

There are three kinds of owl common in the Forest: the Tawny Owl, the Little or French Owl and the Barn Owl. The Barn Owl is now quite rare. The French or Little Owl screeches, the Barn Owl mews but when the Tawny Owl hoots it is a sign of good weather.

The story goes of a man lost in those woods called 'Man lost', the owl hooted 'Hoo, Hoo,' and the man replied 'Tom Morgan from Cinderford.'

———

They mucked the church tower to make it grow high,
But not so lofty as the sky,
And when the muck began to sink
They swore the tower had grown an inch.

This is an old country story from Ebrington in the Cotswolds. Ebrington is known by the local folk as Yubberton and the villagers are called the Yubberton Yawnees. It is a place where outsiders are always taking the mickey out of those who live there. A bit like Mercot Docks, a hamlet near Broadway, where it is said that 'they milk the pigeons for pigeon's milk'.

———

You can tell a Cuckoo a mile away.

This saying means possibly more than meets the eye.

When we speak of the cuckoo we are talking of a bird which puts its eggs into another bird's nest. A cuckold is a man whose wife, to use an old word, is an adulteress. Maybe he too can be spotted a mile away!

It is also said that the cuckoo sucks the eggs of the bird it uses as a foster mother.

William Hathaway, Morris fiddler, at Swell on the Cotswolds, c. 1907

A break from their labours at Bledington for farmers Harry Jefferies and George Cook, c. 1924; Harry's son George holds the dog. Heavy duty cord trousers, gaiters and hob-nail boots attest to hard physical work in the fields

Mr Edmund Wheeler in retirement at Dyers,
Lower Guiting

Outside the GWR station at Chipping Campden. Standing against the door is Ben
Benfield, horse bus driver for the Noel Arms; others include Mr Ladbroke, butcher
(second left), Mr Fairweather, licensee of the Live and Let Live Inn, and Mr
Blakeman, a local character known as 'slap'

He's got a yud (head) as thick as a beetle.

Shakespeare talks of folk being 'beetle headed'. It just means wooden headed, stupid. A beetle is a wooden mallet used for driving stakes into the ground. I have heard this said often.

'He's got beetle brows.'

This is more difficult to imagine. This comes from Langland's *Piers Plowman*, but does not mean what it appears. It has nothing to do with the insect but still refers to the mallet. To be beetle browed is to pucker the eyebrows like the edge of a beetle which is frayed through use.

He's got more in his head than the comb will take out.

I like this as it means that the person is clever and has a head full of knowledge.

He's a nineter at football.

Quite a common saying in the country. The word nineter comes from 'the annointed one'. It is descriptive.

Yud (head) first or nothing.

This is spoken of someone who does not believe in half measures. All or nothing at all. Some folk are like that and they often succeed.

What he knows would fill a book. What he doesn't know would fill a library.

We have all met these know-all folk. They are called by different names, such as 'The block of knowledge', 'clever breeches', 'brains', etc. This is a put-down.

I've never rubbed my back against a college wall.

An old friend of mine who could turn his hand to most things said these words. He was an expect hedgelayer, rick builder, bee keeper, gardener and water diviner. At a parish meeting Joe Baker said this, then added, 'Just because I've had no education folks think that I've got a tile loose.'

The fact was that Joe, despite not having book knowledge, had many skills.

Thee hast been to Beckford.

A local saying used by the folk in my village of Ashton-under-Hill. If someone got a bit above themselves and put on airs it used to be said that they had been to Beckford. Beckford was 2 miles away. The vicar lived there, the police station was there, and at one time a court was held there. The post office there could issue gun licences, etc, and the railway station had facilities for loading cattle and a coal wharf. Beckford also had a market.

Beckford folk therefore felt superior to folk at our village. If you had been to Beckford surely something had rubbed off and you knew a thing or two!

You village chaps be nothing but swede gnawers.

This was said by a villager who had gone away to make his fortune on the railway in Birmingham. When he returned for the weekend he said this in the village pub. Tom, the local thatcher said, 'I'll show you whether I'm a swede-gnawer or not!' and he gave the fellow a good hiding. He added, 'just because we live in a village, that doesn't mean that we all gnaw swedes and eat tallow candles.'

Drunk as a Bob Howler.

This is an expression Tom also used of the Birmingham chap, and very descriptive it is. The Bob Howler is the countryman's name for a big moth which comes out at night. This moth, as it comes from outside on a summer's night into the living room, makes for the lamp. It circles the lamp, burning its wings on the flame as it is mesmerized by the light. A drunken man can be likened to a Bob Howler.

If thou can'st read, write and reckon and think for theeself the gate's open.

Another saying from the Forest of Dean. It may have been true in the past but in today's world 'reading, writing and arithmetic' is not enough.

It is true, some folk with very little technical knowledge do succeed in their work. In the past, there was even some benefit in not being able to write. I knew a man who could not sign a cheque who became very well off. The gate was open and he went through.

Snobbery would die out tomorrow if boot-licking stopped.

Here is something worth thinking about. Boot-licking can be creeping around someone with authority for your own gain. If everyone had dignity, however humble their position in life, instead of the 'Yes, Sir. No, Sir. Three bags full, Sir.' attitude, perhaps snobbery would end.

She looks as if butter wouldn't melt in her mouth, but a good hard lump of cheese wouldn't choke her.

A rather unkind assessment of a person, yet one can be deceived by appearances. Folk like those in the saying are described today as being 'smooth', 'laid back', etc. Some folk can be 'read like a book', others are not so easy to know.

CHAPTER EIGHTEEN

About Guns and Shooting

Up gets seven and sixpence. Bang goes two pence.
Down comes half-a-crown.

This refers to pheasants: they never make as much money when sold as it costs to rear them.

The prices here are from the 1920s when it cost 7s. 6d. to rear a pheasant. The birds in those days were hatched and reared under broody hens. The gamekeeper came around the village and would pay four shillings for a broody hen. After the pheasant poults were reared and the hens were not wanted the gamekeeper sold them for a shilling or so for boiling fowls. Cartridges were 2d. each so 'Bang' went 2d. Half-a-crown was the usual price for a pheasant.

There's another barrel empty and I haven't had a spot.

Here is a saying from our cowman when he heard a gun fired.

Of course he was talking of two sorts of barrels, the gun barrel and the cider barrel. A bit of rustic humour.

In the 1920s at a shoot near where I lived the guns included some city businessmen with expensive Purdy 12-bore hammerless guns. They were not very good marksmen. The local doctor was easily the best shot among the party.

They couldn't hit a barn if they were standing inside.

A derogatory comment made by our cowman of the city gentlemen. Admittedly, it would be difficult to miss the mark in those circumstances!

What sights you see when you haven't got your gun!

Literally this happens on the farm. Many a covey of Partridge have settled in the asparagus bower close to where we were picking the sprouts, when, of course, 'I hadn't got my gun'. But, of course, the saying is meant concerning other sights.

Tom, our cowman, used this saying on many occasions. One lady in the village wore extraordinary hats. In fact Tom reckoned that this one day she was wearing two hats. 'What sights you see when you haven't got your gun!' he would say. Then he would use another of his sayings of wit and wisdom: 'When that hat has puppies I'd like one of them.'

When Jim the coalman came to work one day looking very odd the carter said: 'Whatever have you been doing to your hair?' He replied, 'The missus started to cut it last night and didn't have time to finish it. She's going to finish it tonight.' What a sight!

Farming practice when I was a boy was governed by very strict rules. Mistakes were noticed. For instance, if a field of wheat came up and there were gaps across the crop where the men had gone wide with the drill it stuck out like a sore thumb until harvest. Crooked bean rows, crooked furrows, were the source of harmless talk. How often has a farmer had to put a wooden prop against a leaning rick?

When I grew plums a neighbour of mine, a very good neighbour but eccentric, offered to pick for me. One moonlit night when I went to a stubble field adjoining the plum orchard to shut the fowls up in their arks, I saw something

Arthur Archer, gamekeeper to J.C. Nicklin, in Ashton Wood, 1913

A shooting party in the Cheddar area of Somerset

Doctor Roberson in his trap with Lavender, a London cab horse, by the village cross in Ashton-under-Hill, c. 1880

Mr Court with rabbits caught on Bredon Hill

moving at the top of a plum tree. It was my neighbour picking plums by moonlight. I called to him, 'Good night. Can you see to pick by moonlight?' He replied, 'Yes. It's nice and cool working now.' I thought: 'What sights you see when you haven't got your gun.'

CHAPTER NINETEEN

In the Family

Birds of a feather flock together.

The Starling is a good example of this saying. Robins are not so friendly to each other.

These words applying to people have a ring of truth. It is the herding instinct in us. Men's Clubs, the W.I., etc. and way back in our school days we found our own level with friends.

My Dad as a farmer was not so keen on his workers being too cliquish. It could hinder the work.

It runs in families like wooden legs.

This saying has a subtle meaning. We know wooden legs do not run in families, but certain traits, strengths and weaknesses do appear in families generation after generation.

A family I know, they are friends of mine, are good cricketers, in fact they are excellent cricketers. One branch of the family provided a wicket-keeper for the county. A hundred years ago Edward kept wicket for his village team. Years later his son kept wicket for the same village. Now his grandson is wicket-keeper in the same team and his great-grandson keeps wicket on odd occasions, deputizing for his Dad.

Another family I knew well were all musical except one. The father played the big bass viol, two sons each played violas and the daughter played the organ, the 'cello and the accordion. This musical ability ran in the family. The grandfather also played the fiddle.

A man doesn't wake up his second child just to see it smile.

Here are words of experience! The first child is a novelty. The father sticks to the old adage 'Let sleeping dogs lie' with the second child.

This saying has a wider meaning, in that when things are quiet and comfortable leave well alone.

Stolen sweets are always sweeter.
Stolen kisses much completer.
Stolen looks are nice in chapels.
Stolen, stolen be your apples.

Scrumping apples has always been a weakness with children. However green or sour, there is an achievement in going through a gap in the hedge. The same goes for these first stolen kisses!

There's been more bones made on Bredon Hill than have been broken.

Here is a skittish saying I heard said by the old men, men who were old when I was a boy. They would, perhaps with a certain envy, see a young courting couple going up the hill in the summer on a Sunday afternoon. This was known as 'The Mac Carrying Season' when young hopefuls took a mac up on the hill as a mattress for their love-making. Bones have been made on Bredon as on other hills and moors. Some are men and women today and are a credit to the hill villages.

Bones *have* been broken on Bredon, but it is now more than a hundred years since Lady Coventry fell from her horse near the cuckoo pen and broke her leg. She was hunting with the Croome Hounds. Her horse broke its back as it jumped a fairly low wall with a deep drop on the other side.

The cuckoo pen is a group of fenced in Beech trees on Little Hill. The idea was that if the cuckoo could be penned we would have spring and summer all the year round.

***

When you marry, marry a big woman and live in a small house, you won't need much furniture.

Here's how our cowman Tom advised me. I did start married life in a small house, but not with a big woman! The war was on and our furniture was 'utility' and some second-hand. I do not think anyone would take Tom seriously when choosing a partner, or a house.

***

That was before I bought my shovel.

Another saying of Jack the carpenter, which signified that he was speaking of long ago when he was what he called a 'hobbledehoy', neither man nor boy, a teenager in modern speech. It was talking in riddles, but it explains the innocence of youth.

***

Stock is as good as money.

Folk with large families used to say this and there was a certain amount of truth in the saying. Close knit families when, as the saying goes, 'Blood is thicker than water', did look after their parents when they became old and kept them from the dreaded workhouse.

CHAPTER TWENTY

Pub Sayings

As a bird is known by its note so is a man known by his conversation.

Swearing strictly prohibited.

This legend is on the wall at the Star Inn, Ashton-under-Hill. The landlord of the pub in Grandfather's day was a religious man and had this notice on the wall for his customers. He would not allow card playing in the bar on Sundays.

Jack, the rough carpenter, one of his regulars, who always started his drinking with a quart, was a character. One night he looked across the room at the bar at two mugs on the shelf opposite. He said: 'Those two mugs are just alike, especially that one.' The men would brag about their eyesight. One said: 'I've just seen a fly on Broadway Monument' (6 miles away). Jack replied, 'I've just seen him wink his eye.'

'I looks towards ya.'
'I catches yer eye.'
'I speaks according.'
'I bows and smiles.'

This toast said thousands of times in local pubs is very old. It is said when a villager buys a drink for his friend. His friend says, 'I looks towards ya', and so on.

In the Cotswolds my old friend Fred will insist on buying me a drink. 'Have one with me,' he would say.

'I'll just have a half,' I would reply. Fred would return from the bar with a pint. I would say, 'That's a big half-pint, Fred.'

His reply, I thought, was a gem. It is so original. I am fond of hearing it. It is: 'A bird never flew with half a wing.'

No, a bird does not fly with half a wing, which is the reason, of course, for clipping just one wing on domestic fowl.

After a while I would say: 'You'd better have a drink with me, Fred.'

He would reply: 'I'll chance another.'

―――――

Here's to the two things in life I love best, a good horse and a pretty woman.

Another toast heard in a country pub. The full toast goes: 'When I die I don't want to be buried, I want to be skinned and my skin tanned and made into a saddle. A lady's saddle indeed. And when I am dead and long since gone I shall rest between the two things in life I loved best, a good horse and a pretty woman.'

―――――

Beer on cider is not a good rider.
Cider on beer makes you very queer.

This, another saying of my old friend, is true I believe. It is something I have not had personal experience of. There must be some truth in the saying because to mix drinks of a barley and apple kind is similar to mixing grain with grape.

Tetbury Ted on a horse outside The Plough and Harrow, Ashton-under-Hill, with landlord William Hooper, 1920

The Star Inn, Ashton-under-Hill

Threshing the allotment holders' ricks in the yard of The Plough and Harrow

Patience and water gruel are good for the gout.

Gout is said to be caused by drinking too much alcohol. The saying suggests that by living frugally, drinking what it says – water gruel – and having patience, gout can be cured.

I remember a gentleman who was with me at the Turkish baths being badly affected with gout. I asked the masseur, 'Can you cure this gentleman?'

He replied, 'Yes, if he would cooperate and moderate his drinking.'

CHAPTER TWENTY-ONE

Among the Hedgerows

Beware the Oak it draws a stroke.
Avoid the Ash it courts the flash.
Creep under the thorn it will keep you from harm.

Here is a countryman's advice on sheltering from a thunderstorm.

A thorn bush is not so tall as an Oak or Ash tree. Lightning strikes the highest object in a field, so the trees draw the flash. In a cricket field when the players are the highest objects they are at risk from lightning.

Country folk in their cottages have in the past turned mirrors against the wall and put away knives and forks, they were reputed to draw the lightning.

———

It's as if he had found a titty obin's nest and is laughing at the ballchins.

I have heard this said of someone who seems very pleased about something.

The titty obin is the little Robin, the ballchins are the unfledged young birds in the nest, bald chicks. I suppose children would laugh at the poor helpless little bald robins in a nest. It is an old saying, a bit of a riddle.

A fish and a friend are good for three days.

It is true that a fish will go bad after three days and will not be fit to eat. This is a pessimistic statement to make about friendship. We have all heard of 'fair weather friends' who do not last, but three days is a very short friendship.

As slick or sleek as an 'oont'.

The oont is the Gloucestershire name for a mole. Their hills are oonty tumps. Moles' coats are sleek. The skins used to be in demand by the furriers.

The expression above was often used by Dad's partner, Mr Bailey, when he described cattle that were thriving. As slick as oonts. The opposite for plain cattle was 'As thin as hurdles'.

The grass is always greener the other side of the hedge.

This refers to sheep or cattle which get restless when they are always in the same field, but also describes those who always see a better opportunity elsewhere.

What isn't too hot for him isn't too heavy.

A saying about someone who is light-fingered, or unscrupulous.

What will keep the cold out will keep the heat out.

In the 1930s tramps walked along the main road from one workhouse to another. Even in hot weather they would wear overcoats while we were working in the field in shirt sleeves. Cousin George said this to me. It may be true, for some people in hot countries do wear a lot of clothes.

CHAPTER TWENTY-TWO

Whatever Will Be Will Be

It's always been the same since Adam was a boy.

This was Ralph, our carter's, favourite expression. Things did not always go just right with horses and implements. The rains came down, the clay stuck to the mould board of the plough, one of the plough mares would be what Ralph called 'in use', in season, and would jib and kick over the traces. Ralph knew that his thirty shillings wage would not allow him beer, only tobacco, when the housekeeping had to be paid. For as season followed season, as his horses got older, so did Ralph, and ever since Adam was a boy it has been the same.

We shall have to send for that man from London.

Ralph would say this when the binder did not tie the sheaves tidily and we tried to adjust the knotter.

I asked, 'Who was he then?' Ralph replied, 'There's a man up in London who knows everything and can make and mend anything. There is a wonderful man in London, I wish he was here to mend this knotter.'

That's the certain truth and the truth needs no study.

This was said to me by what was known as a rough carpenter on the farm, a maker of rough gates called heavers, a mender of wagon shafts, etc. It is a statement that if one speaks the truth there should be no problem, unlike a liar who has to have a good memory.

They always give an apple where there is an orchard.

This is often true in life. For instance, if a raffle is held and the prize is a box of fruit the person who wins it has plenty in the orchard. The really needy rarely get any extras. A legacy from a will goes to someone or some organization with plenty of money. They always give an apple where there is an orchard.

Picture Acknowledgements

The author and publisher would like to thank the following for permission to reproduce photographs: The Museum of English Rural Life, University of Reading, pp. xiib bottom, 4b, 14b, 20a top, 26a top, 50b top, 74b top, 80a bottom, 92a bottom; Cotswold Countryside Collection at Northleach (Cotswold District Council), pp. 26b bottom, 30a, 30b, 38a bottom, 44b top and bottom, 50a top and bottom, 50b bottom, 56a, 56b top and bottom, 62a bottom (courtesy of Gloucestershire Record Office), 70a bottom (courtesy of Hereford City Library), 70b bottom, 74a top and bottom, 86a top (courtesy of English Folk Dance and Song Society) and bottom, 86b top and bottom; Oxfordshire County Council: Department of Leisure and Arts, pp. 4a (courtesy of Cotswold Countryside Collection at Northleach), 14a top.